CLAUDE MORIN

Quebec versus Ottawa:
the struggle for self-government
1960-72

Translated from *Le Pouvoir québécois... en négociation* and
from *Le Combat québécois* by RICHARD HOWARD

UNIVERSITY OF TORONTO PRESS
Toronto Buffalo London

Original French editions
Le Pouvoir québécois . . . en négotiation © 1972 and
Le Combat québécois © 1973
by Les Editions du Boréal Express,
2385 rue Chapleau, Sillery, Québec

English edition
©University of Toronto Press 1976
Toronto   Buffalo   London
Reprinted 1978

Library of Congress Cataloging in Publication Data

Morin, Claude, 1929 -
    Quebec versus Ottawa.

    1. Quebec (Province) — Politics and government —
    1960- 2. Federal government—Canada. I. Howard,
    Richard Christopher, 1940-   II. Morin, Claude,
    1929- Le combat québecois. English. 1976.
    III. title.
    JL246.S8M6713   320.9'714'04   76-16163
    ISBN 0-8020-2166-2
    ISBN 0-8020-6249-0 pbk.

CLAUDE MORIN was appointed Minister of Intergovernmental Affairs for Quebec following the election of the Parti québécois government in 1976.

From 1963 to 1971, during a period that witnessed growing stress and strain in Quebec's relations with the federal government, Claude Morin was Deputy Minister of Intergovernmental Affairs in Quebec.

In setting forth his point of view on many of the issues and conflicts with Ottawa, from the pension plan to the constitutional conferences, this book should help English-speaking Canadians to an understanding of the Québécois ideas of federalism during these years and of how people in Quebec can come to believe that sovereignty is essential.

Quebec versus Ottawa is an edited and updated translation by Richard Howard of *Le Pouvoir québécois . . . en négotiation*, published in French in 1972, and of *Le Combat québécois* (1973). It thus has two parts, 'Experience,' dealing more with the facts of Quebec-Ottawa relations during the troubled sixties, and 'Answers,' describing the structure and rules of Canadian federalism as the author experienced them.

M. Morin is not presenting arguments for the independence of Quebec but is rather recording and evaluating his experience of how our government works - a rare thing for a senior civil servant to do.

The dialectic of master and slave works in the political sphere in such a way that the victor compels the vanquished, not only to accept his vision of the world, but also to adopt the formulae by which he shall utter his own capitulation. In other words, the vanquished in the game of politics is he who allows the attitude of the other to be imposed on him, and judges his own acts with the adversary's eyes.

Karel Kočik

Contents

A Note on the Translation

Claude Morin's *Le Pouvoir québécois ... en négociation* and *Le Combat québécois* (herein combined and edited) were written as a kind of extramural course in federal-provincial relations for a community in which these affairs intrigue, and mystify, a wide public. The books' aim implied an extensive use of documentation and illustration as well as a strong pattern of summary and restatement — elements which it was not thought necessary to reproduce unscathed in an English-language edition. M. Morin's analyses and conclusions are, however, retained here without alteration.

RH

Preface to the English Edition

My personal experience of over eight years in federal-provincial relations had prompted a number of observations and judgements that might, it seemed to me, be usefully shared with my fellow Québécois. So it was that shortly after leaving my post as deputy minister of Intergovernmental Affairs for Quebec, I began drafts of the two volumes which appeared in 1972 and 1973.

It gave me great pleasure, and pride as well, obviously, to learn of the intention of the University of Toronto Press to translate these two books.

The decision is especially gratifying to me as it will give a concerned public in English Canada an opportunity to judge for themselves how at variance the Québécois' ideas of federalism, the role of central government, and the position of the provinces can frequently be with their own. This will probably help them identify the sources of certain federal-provincial conflicts, and the reasons underlying the Quebec-Ottawa differences that at intervals during these last few years have troubled the whole of Canada.

Contrary to what some might expect, my two books, made into a single volume and brought up to date for the present edition, do not constitute a plea for Quebec independence. They do provide an explanation why, however, from his experience of the concrete every-day working of the federal system, a Québécois can come to believe that sovereignty is essential.

There are two parts to the present volume. The first of them offers a factual analysis of the Quebec-Ottawa 'cases' of greatest consequence in the years 1960-72. The second contains a study of the Canadian governmental structure and the rules by which our federal system is bound. In the first of these parts as much as in the second I have attempted to be as objective as possible, choosing my ground in every case on provable fact. Objectivity, however, does not mean neutrality, and so I have felt obliged to accept those conclusions that seemed to me dictated by realities observed at first hand.

Finally, my hope is that this book will afford readers an opportunity to better understand Quebec's recent evolution and its attitude to federalism.

Claude Morin
Quebec City
December 1975

PART 1
EXPERIENCES

1
The Gains of the Sixties:
What were They?

There was a view, particularly current after 1964, that recent developments in the federal system of Canada had opened the way for the government of Quebec to make a number of so-called 'gains'. Through negotiation, Quebec had won control over new and important areas of governmental action and taken advantage of substantial improvements in the distribution of fiscal and financial resources between Ottawa and the provinces. It was further held that the federal structure under which we operate in no way acted as an obstacle to the present powers of Quebec, or indeed to any it might manage to secure.

Once this truth had dawned on us, we would naturally have better use for our energies than to revise a constitution already proven flexible by experience. There would be even less call to reject a political system which not only accommodates all Quebec's aspirations but also, through the healthy competition it stimulates between governments, lends a dynamism to the whole governing process. To convinced federalists, the achievement of these gains seemed to stand as corroboration of the advantages of the present political system, its wealth of adaptability, its potential for the future.

In following chapters, some of the more significant and well known of these gains are analyzed in their true context. I will not be dealing with Quebec's 'losses' in the same period, although in number they were just as great as the advances that so many admire.

The story really begins with the not-so-quiet 'Quiet Revolution.' After a period of tough negotiation, merciless debate, unprecedented tension, and even an ultimatum in 1963 from Quebec's prime minister, Jean Lesage, the following year at last witnessed the first substantial breakthrough in federal-provincial relations since that revolution had begun. Several large issues came up simultaneously for exhaustive discussion: the pension plan, the shared cost programs, and the resource transfer to the provinces.

The process continued as, in 1965, Quebec signed agreements with Paris in culture and education. Later, in 1968 and 1969, an arrangement was worked out with Ottawa that allowed Quebec to take part in international conferences on education, an exclusively provincial jurisdiction. In 1967, Quebec had arranged for the provincial housing corporation to become the unique avenue for loans and subsidies from the federal Central Mortgage and Housing Corporation to reach public housing and urban renewal projects in Quebec. Meanwhile the Canada Assistance Plan was set up with strong inspiration from Quebec research studies and accommodating the philosophy Quebec wanted to bring into its income support programs at the time. Federal regional development programs too bore the imprint of Quebec thinking. Again because of Quebec, the central administration grew increasingly involved with the Francophone world community and evolved a broad policy of bilingualism. In 1968, Quebec had at last convinced the rest of Canada of the urgent need for constitutional review. The process was launched amid numerous encounters of government leaders and experts from all over the country.

Many lesser instances could be cited in the same vein. Putting them all together, we could draw an inspiring picture to show how the federal system has never stopped Quebec from getting along and gaining acceptance for its view — indeed, demonstrate the contrary. It is a mere step from this to the intimation that equally spectacular advances are always possible, if only we can put our faith in federalism and learn to make use of all its advantages. This step is all the more easily taken since, time and time again, Ottawa spokesmen and their allies in Quebec go back to this fund of presumed or possible gains for the arguments they use on Quebeckers who, taught to fear any major change in the Canadian political system, are often all too happy to believe them. An example of this was the federal pamphlet entitled *Quoi de neuf?* extolling the system's immense financial advantages for Quebec: hard-hitting despite its gross errors, the publication was circulated at the close of the provincial election campaign of April 1970.

In federal-provincial affairs, as in any other area, incomplete knowledge of the situation as a whole, or of its historical background, often prevents us from taking the true measure of certain realities. The Quebecker's attention will be invited to one gain or another achieved in the past ten or twelve years without any explanation of why it was possible, what improvement it brought about, or how, in the middle and long term, it helps increase or consolidate the real powers of the government of Quebec.

Close study of the gains listed above reveals a picture much less idyllic than the one put forward by official interpreters of the Canadian reality. As we will see in the chapters that follow, Quebec's gains in the federal context during these past few years have been all in all rather slim. This assertion may be surprising: we are used to thinking that the period has been full of definite advances for Quebec, much-discussed advances which are supposed to have come from the new energy of the Quiet Revolution and an understanding attitude on the federal government's part.

In this analysis, my criterion has been the extent to which the powers of the Quebec government were confirmed and, especially, extended in conflict with Ottawa. In short, changes in the relative situation of Quebec strike me as positive and well directed to the extent that by them its government is strengthened juridically, financially, and politically. Thus I do not see as a 'gain' the Ottawa takeover of programs previously paid for by Quebec City, even if it results in a saving for the latter or an increase of a few thousand dollars in federal grants to Quebec for shared cost programs; such cases are in fact often accompanied by a loss of power in the sense described.

But why make the confirmation and extension of the powers of Quebec's government my criterion in evaluating the development of federal-provincial relations? Is there no other way to measure Quebec's progress than on the political plane? Why found our entire analysis on the idea of gains? Why stress one institution, the Quebec government, and not the others?

In fact there are various ways of evaluating Quebec's progress over the last few years in terms of resource development, the standard of living of its citizens, the quality of life, or the exploitation of its wealth. But alternatives are fewer when it comes to evaluating the development of federalism; and attention is directed specifically to recent developments in our political system. We must also bear in mind that it is in these recent years that the federal system was more systematically and insistently challenged than ever before. We must determine why this has been so. In the official Ottawa version, the unease of Quebec arose from the feeling of its people that they were not at home in the rest of Canada and also from their inadequate rate of economic growth: hence the policies of bilingualism and regional development.

According to Quebec, there exists another diagnosis and another prescription. Like many other peoples, Quebeckers have experienced an awakening of self-consciousness. They want to assert themselves, not as French-speaking Canadians, but as Québécois, citizens who, for the moment, suffer the want of a country that is their own. In this perspective, their government becomes a means of action, a lever, a collective tool, and the only one Quebeckers can at this point control completely themselves. We must not forget that the Quebec problem is sociological, psychological, and political, as well as economic. Put this way it is more difficult to define, but one truth remains: whether or not Canada becomes officially more bilingual, whether or not the sums available for regional development are increased, the problem of Quebec will not thereby be solved.

It can be claimed that the yardstick of Quebec gains is not entirely relevant in evaluating the recent trend of Canadian federalism, since any advance occurred in the context of a given division of powers between Ottawa and the provinces, a division that only amendment of the constitution can change. The fact is, moreover, that most Quebec-Ottawa negotiations, except of course in the process of constitutional review itself, were not aimed at transformation of the political structure.

This may well be true, but if it is we should always have heard it loud and clear that Quebec could not hope for any new powers. The contrary has been the case: we have been given to believe that Canadian federalism affords Quebec all the freedom it wants to consolidate and increase its powers by the strength and quality of its arguments. Since the issue has been raised in terms of powers, this is the concept on which I will base my evaluation of Quebec's political advance since 1960.

2
A Beginning: The Pension Plan

The throne speech of 16 May 1963 advertised the federal government's intention of bringing into being a universal, contributory pension plan. The plan was to facilitate the mobility of Canadians while at the same time guaranteeing them greater income security.

At that point Quebec was casting around for financial resources both readily accessible and suited to speed up implementation of a number of new government programs. Beginning in 1960 we had, contrary to previous policy, gone heavily into public borrowing. At all events, a diversification of money sources was necessary in view of the multitude of programs aimed at making up for time lost under the former administration.

Specifically, some had envisaged finding a way to tap the immense reservoir of capital that could result from citizens' contributions to a public pension plan. There had already been reports in this vein from the civil service. The 1962 election platform of the Union nationale, without going so far as to propose a state-administered fund, emphasized portability among the various pension schemes, an aim not fully attainable except with government involvement.

In short, the notion of a fund under government supervision was beginning to hatch, and it was increasingly obvious that public retirement insurance or something of the sort would be the best way, as well as the quickest, of assuring abundant capital for this fund. Quebec politicians and officials in France as observers had been much impressed by the Caisse de dépôts et de consignations and the substantial contribution that institution made to the French economy. Preliminary study at home had revealed that the amounts assigned to such a fund would soon rise into the hundreds of millions of dollars and even exceed a billion if the rate of contribution were high enough. It must be pointed out, however, that at this time — May 1963 — almost no solid technical studies had been carried out in Quebec on either a possible development fund or a pension scheme. The ideas were around, attracting attention from various individuals in the absence of any precise government directive in the area.

The news of a federal pension arrangement, valid for all Canada and run by Ottawa, came as a dire blow to Quebec's half-formed resolve to move in the same field, particularly since the federal plan made no provision for accruing large money reserves. This Ottawa program was to be funded as it went along, with contributions rising as greater numbers of subscribers moved into retirement. Yet for Quebec to achieve its aim of controlling large amounts of capital, it was essential for the plan to be administered directly by the province and, in contrast to the federal scheme, provide for an immediate accumulation of funds.

It is thus readily understandable that Ottawa and Quebec should soon emerge in opposition to one another across the whole pensions area. Ottawa's plan had been bruited publicly, and its technical supporting studies were definitely more advanced than Quebec's, two factors that gave the federal government a starting advantage. Quebec City quickly began to move. During the summer of 1963, Claude Castonguay, then a consulting actuary, worked with an interdepartmental committee to complete the first draft of Quebec's pension-scheme project, basically similar to the one now in existence. The same process brought into focus another project, logically linked to the pension plan: the Quebec Deposit and Investment Fund.

There is no need at this point to go into detail on the ins and outs of Quebec-Ottawa dealings arising from the conflict between proponents of the two plans. Let me merely say that after the tense and eventful federal-provincial conference in Quebec City during March and April 1964, compromise was reached between the two governments: Ottawa would take to the rest of the country what was for all practical purposes the plan proposed by Quebec, while Quebec set up its own independent scheme.

This arrangement was welcomed at the time as a resounding victory for co-operative federalism and mutual understanding. It is invoked occasionally even today to show us how all things are possible in federalism. Yet how much truth is there in this claim?

In practical terms the compromise undoubtedly suited Quebec by opening the way for full satisfaction of its immediate aims. No one can deny that Quebec kept all the freedom it wanted in this area. Most particularly it could, as intended, make use of the amounts gathered through the pension plan and handed over to the Deposit and Investment Fund. Nor should it be forgotten that Quebec's establishment of a universal, compulsory, and public pension plan was aided by Ottawa's prior decision to do the same thing. We must realize that private insurance firms and, in a general way, what we usually call 'big business' took a less than ecstatic view of such a 'socialist' innovation. History will never reveal with absolute clarity whether Quebec would have been dogged enough on its own to go ahead with a measure whose state-controlled complexion was so sourly met in financial circles. Given the mood of the Quiet Revolution it is probable that it would have done so, but counter-pressure would still have been enormous.

The federal government managed at the same time to get what it wanted — the establishment of a large-scale program in an area of provincial priority — since the other provinces went along with the move. In time, by successive constitutional amendments and the use of its spending power, Ottawa had procured for itself a measure of jursidiction in the field of income support. That field had originally been placed under general provincial power, until the later section 94A of the British North America Act gave the federal authorities a parallel power, though not a priority one, to pass laws on old age pensions and supplementary benefits. In setting up a pension plan for nine provinces Ottawa consolidated its position in social policy and sited a stepping-stone for the future. Nor does Quebec's plan being taken away from the central administration at the outset in any sense alter the fact that all Canadians were henceforth under uniform protection, something for which Ottawa could later claim the credit as occasion arose.

At the time of the pension debate Ottawa thus managed to have the scope of section 94A enlarged. From then on its parallel non-priority power would extend, for example, to needy mothers' allowances, an area until then wholly in provincial hands. Quebec agreed to the constitutional amendment on the understanding that it would organize its own pensions and contract out, with compensation, from new shared cost programs under the altered section 94A; the new scope of the section, therefore, would not necessarily seem to affect Quebec. In setting up the Quebec Pension Plan, on the other hand, Quebec conquered no new constitutional territory, but simply occupied a field of its own that Ottawa had been preparing to mine.

One lesson people have tried to extract from the establishment of the Quebec Pension Plan has to do with the great flexibility of Canadian federalism. Why complain, they say, about a political system that does not force a province to apply a 'national' program it sees as unsuitable, but rather lets it go its own way? A few points need to be made in reply.

The 'national' program put forward by the central authorities covered an area where provincial jurisdiction could apply. In the circumstances, we might rather think the Canadian political system flexible particularly in Ottawa's favour, since it admitted the federal government to provincial preserves. Moreover, the Quebec plan was and still is absolutely identical to that run by Ottawa. During the 1964 Ottawa-Quebec negotiations virtually everything was done to ensure a flawless resemblance between the two. Quebec agreed to abandon some of the features it wanted in its plan: a longer transition period, a different rate of payment, and so on. Ottawa, for its part, recognized the Quebec project's superiority and went even farther in deciding, once it had been slightly modified, to apply it to the whole country. It would certainly be intriguing to know what Ottawa's reaction would be if Quebec decided unilaterally, as it has a perfect right to do, to make radical alterations in the Quebec Pension Plan. Only in such a case could we see how far Quebec's latitude really extends.

Although the Quebec-Ottawa arrangement of 1964 was greeted as a most reasonable one, it left some bitterness in Ottawa, along with a persistent yearning for complete federal control over public retirement insurance schemes throughout Canada. Though the two plans were initially identical, there was still the danger, more in theory than otherwise, that Canadians could one day be confronted by a variety of provincial systems. In this contingency the federal people saw a potentially serious obstacle to the mobility of Canadians, who would face losing either their right to a pension or else established financial advantages if they relocated in a province with lower pension levels. Their concern, which was probably sincere, masked yet another federal anxiety. To back up its approach to retirement insurance and pensions, Quebec had relied on a constitutional paramountcy that went more or less unchallenged at the time. Even in July 1963, when the Quebec scheme was still being worked out, Prime Minister Jean Lesage expressly told a federal-provincial conference that Quebec would not accept the federal plan, and would fulfil its responsibility by setting up its own scheme. His position was reiterated in the Quebec brief to the federal-provincial conference of November 1963: 'It has been known since the month of July that Quebec refuses to have the federal plan applied to its citizens. We have chosen in this case to stick to the option formula, and will institute a public, universal, and actuarially-based provincial plan.'

Ottawa's meditations on constitutional review had elicited the fact that in this area the BNA Act harboured a flaw which could harm its discretionary power of intervention in issues of 'national interest.' According to the federal government, the mobility of all Canadians was such an issue; the argument was there, at least, to be trotted out whenever the conjuncture, political or otherwise, seemed right for correcting the 'anomaly' that had let Quebec set up an independent pension plan. A 1969 working paper on constitutional review, entitled *Income Security and Social Services*, gave Ottawa its chance to issue a clear statement of how, precisely, it would have preferred the Canadian constitution to clarify federal powers in favour of the central administration. As the working paper stated: 'The Government of Canada has concluded that the best course would be to put Parliament in a position to provide leadership in the field of public retirement insurance. For this purpose Parliament and the provincial legislatures ought to continue to have concurrent powers in respect of public retirement insurance and associated benefits, but Parliament's powers should be paramount (in the case of conflict between federal and provincial plans the federal plan would prevail).'

Consider for a moment the tactical aspect of this federal proposal. In practical terms it could lead to Ottawa's repossession of the Quebec Pension Plan. Despite all the working paper's rhetorical precautions, I can give it no other interpretation. The proposal probably was not conceived for this purpose alone, but the Quebec plan undoubtedly served as a frame of reference for the paper's authors.

The proposal remained simply that, however. When it turned up on the agenda of the premiers' constitutional conference of September 1970, Quebec fought it for obvious reasons. Quebec negotiators made the counter-suggestion of putting in its place, with no alteration in the current division of powers, a clause providing that the exercise of the various governments' prerogatives in the field must necessarily respect the compatibility of the different public retirement insurance schemes. Other provinces, notably Ontario, echoed Quebec's stand, and in any case the suspension of constitutional review in June 1971 meant that the Ottawa proposal went no farther. Nothing, however, discourages me from expecting it to turn up again one of these days.

3

A Liberty Surveyed:
The Shared Cost Programs

At the federal-provincial conference of July 1960, Quebec Prime Minister Jean Lesage proposed an end to well-established shared cost programs, with compensation to provinces in the amount of the conditional grants Ottawa had been paying for the programs up to that time. Before Lesage, Maurice Duplessis had repeatedly denounced these programs, by and large for the same reasons argued in the Tremblay Report: federal interference in provincial preserves, lack of respect for provincial priorities, constant federal inspection, and so on. It was a stand that prompted Duplessis' rejection of conditional grants from Ottawa to the extent they affected, as they said in those days, the 'autonomy and rights of the province.'

Noting the loss of grant moneys other provinces were collecting, Lesage decided that Quebec, without prejudice to his call for withdrawal, would participate in several of these shared cost programs until the issue was resolved: this was the case, for instance, with the hospital insurance his Liberals were committed to bring in for Quebec after the 1960 election. 'These circumstances have obliged Quebec to adhere to a number of shared cost programs since 1960,' the premier would announce in his opening remarks to the federal-provincial gathering of March and April 1964: 'At the same time we have never viewed this compliance as anything more than a temporary expedient until the problem is satisfactorily resolved.'

The Quebec stand on shared cost programs was reiterated at each such conference. It grew to be far more than merely a general assertion, and emerged with particular insistence at the spring 1964 meeting. Mr Lesage's opening statement at that conference contained a specific suggestion on the mechanism of withdrawal. It must be kept in mind that Quebec pressure during the 1963 election campaign had prompted federal Liberals to accept the general principle of opting out of 'well-established' programs. That position had little to say, however, in terms of detail, and it embraced all provinces without distinction.

The spring 1964 conference, toughest so far of the sixties, ended in deadlock. The governments — in reality Ottawa and Quebec City — did not agree on either the federal plan for universal pensions or the winding up of shared cost programs, or even tax sharing. All these issues survived for intense Quebec-Ottawa discussion, ending in a variety of arrangements that together made up a sort of 'package deal.' In the preceding chapter we saw how the pension dilemma was resolved. On the shared cost programs Ottawa accepted the principle of contracting out; technical follow-up negotiations brought officials together in the months of May and June 1964.

By 15 August Lester Pearson, then prime minister of Canada, was finally able to make Lesage an offer. During a transition period lasting from 1965 to 1970 in the case of most programs, and from 1965 to 1967 for some lesser ones, Ottawa's participation in hospital insurance, old age assistance, and blind and disabled persons allowances, as well as in vocational training and health programs, would be replaced by a fiscal abatement of 20 points of personal income tax. Of these 20 points 14 would apply to hospital insurance, two to old age assistance as well as blindness and disability allowances, two to the welfare component of unemployment insurance, and one point each to the other programs. This fiscal equivalence was to be filled out by cash payments in such a way that tax points plus payments would be precisely equal to the sums the federal government would have authorized for Quebec in the case of no withdrawal. Certain shared cost programs of minor importance were replaced by a simple financial equivalence, that is, involved no supplementary fiscal abatement.

I might add that certain other shared cost programs of a temporary nature or else having to do with research were not included in the option to contract out. Used for programs of too short duration, the equivalence, fiscal or financial, would have given rise to serious administrative complications. The option was closed to research programs since in those cases Ottawa was set on maintaining a direct federal presence. The official reason advanced for its approach, however, was that the costs of these programs varied greatly from year to year. In the circumstances it was impossible, said the federal people, to work out an accurate enough equivalence.

The proposal was put to Quebec in a way that left it open to all provinces, in principle as interested in pulling out of shared cost programs as was Quebec. It is hardly necessary to point out that this was not at all the case, as proven by the rest of the negotiations, but the federal government wanted to avoid the impression that Quebec was getting special treatment.

It was understood in Mr Pearson's August letter that during the whole transition period the shared cost programs from which a province was withdrawing, and for which an equivalence was being worked out, would continue unchanged. In other words, to get the fiscal or financial equivalence Quebec would be bound to maintain shared cost programs in their present form, and put up with the visits of federal inspectors, as before, to see how Quebec's programs were conforming to standards applied over the country as a whole.

Quebec's contracting out of the shared cost programs was characterized at the time, along with the establishment of the Quebec Pension Plan, as a great triumph for co-operative federalism. A fuss was made about the intelligence of such an arrangement and the parties to it lauded for their enlightened pragmatism. Yet again, within a manifestly flexible federal system, Quebec could do as it wished without other provinces suffering any loss and without jeopardizing the 'national objectives.'

We may now wonder exactly what advantages this withdrawal from shared cost programs did bring Quebec. Only one: there was a change in the form of Ottawa's financial participation. Now, rather than simply receiving cheques from Ottawa, Quebec could itself collect an increased number of points of personal income tax. The federal government had vacated the desired fiscal territory. At the same time the terms governing the shared cost programs were preserved in their entirety. Until contracting out was complete, Quebec had no new room for manoeuvre. Given the view that the transition period was intended to supply the time necessary to calculate, from experience, the final equivalence values, the maintenance of identical programs was perfectly acceptable, and in fact Quebec itself had envisaged such a period, proposing first (April 1964) a duration of two years. Since cost trends could not be predicted with accuracy, both sides ended by agreeing to a transition period of five years for the hospital insurance, old age assistance, and blind and disabled persons allowances. It was nevertheless essential to get assurances that there would actually be an end to the period, and that afterwards, when the final equivalence had been calculated, Quebec's room for manoeuvre would be substantially enlarged. The Quebec government thought at the time that it had guarantees enough.

Let us turn now to see what happened when the time came for an understanding with Ottawa on Quebec's final abandonment of the programs. Quebec negotiators always clearly told their federal opposite numbers that the exercise of the right to contract out only made sense to the extent that it pointed to complete independence in these areas. Moreover, statements by Quebec public men left no doubt that they were looking for as much freedom of manoeuvre as possible. Finally, in his August 1964 letter to Prime Minister Lesage, Pearson wrote that 'more permanent arrangements relating to the application of the option formula would be subject to further negotiation at the appropriate time.'

In October 1969, Quebec made its suggestion for a final arrangement and detailed its proposal in official meetings. From the opening of discussion it seemed obvious that the federal government wanted the transition period extended. More specifically, Ottawa was not at all anxious to see a final contracting-out formula settled at that time. The federal people challenged Quebec's technical data, while claiming that absolute withdrawal was hard to envisage. In fact, according to them, experience had revealed the length of the transition period as inadequate to allow accurate forward costing for certain programs that by mutual consent had been modified occasionally since 1965; fiscal reforms planned by Ottawa would alter the bases for calculating the product of the various taxes; and finally, constitutional review could lead to legislative attributions different from those on which Quebec's 1964 stand had been founded. For all these reasons Ottawa preferred to prolong transition by a year, perhaps two. It was a view Quebec had to accept, especially as there were those among its ministers and officials who laid great stress on the substantial risk involved in total withdrawal on the date originally set. During 1970, a Quebec-Ottawa agreement prolonged transition to early 1972.

The final-withdrawal issue came up again at the premiers' conference of November 1971, with the 1972 deadline drawing near. Like all the conferences, this one had been preceded by negotiation at the ministerial and high civil service levels. Once again, it was soon obvious that the federal government was moving towards a further extension. In pre-conference discussion Ottawa had submitted a fresh formula for financing shared cost programs. This formula, however, devised against a background of increasing federal anxiety over central spending, was aimed much more at limiting the federal contribution to the programs, to begin with 1969-70 as the base fiscal year and continue in step with the growth of the Gross National Product, than it was at working out an agreement that could bring about a final equivalence.

The result was a new deadline, set this time for early 1974. In April 1973, Ottawa suggested federal withdrawal from the hospital and health insurance programs: there would be compensation based on a percentage of personal income tax plus the entire revenue in sales and excise taxes from alcoholic beverages and tobacco. There was no suggestion, however, of abandoning the joint character of the Canada Assistance Plan, which would have its role to play in projected reforms in the area of income security. The federal offer, partial in any case compared to the whole range of shared cost programs, was rejected by the provinces, who were worried that they might lose by it financially. Thus the transition period, initially supposed to last from 1965 to 1970, will continue until at least 1977. The Quebec government did not offer particularly strong opposition in 1971, preferring, it seems, the serenity of a new transition period under the guarantee that a large proportion of its expenses would still be borne by Ottawa, to the risk, a fairly limited one, of having to shoulder its full constitutional responsibility in return for a conclusive settlement. We were witnessing an instance of Ottawa's determination not to give up its power of intervention in provincial preserves being indirectly supported by a government in Quebec that was less than eager to press for completion of the recovery drive begun in 1964.

If Quebec had taken a firmer line, could it have completed the drive? Probably not, since Ottawa had never been and still is not in the least inclined to leave the provinces — in this case Quebec — free to act as they wish in jointly run programs. At the premiers' conference of November 1971, Ontario declared its intention of following the route taken by Quebec in 1964. The stand was not unexpected; that province's representatives had hinted at it repeatedly. Ontario could see financial advantages in contracting out of the shared cost programs, first in the possibility of more control over their cost and then in a fiscal abatement allowing that province to 'repatriate' tax points for fiscal revenue that might prove greater, given Ontario's economic situation, than the value of federal participation in the programs at the end of the period of transition. Ottawa's response was instantly negative: in 1964, Quebec had been alone in taking advantage of a proposal open to all provinces, and it was no part of federal policy to reiterate the offer now in 1971. According to the federal government, experience clearly showed the process of contracting out to be much more complex, and attended by consequences for the running of the federal and provincial administrations that were far more grave, than had at first been foreseen. Technical obstacles were raised as well. The truth is that in the federal view it was unthinkable to let Ontario follow Quebec at this late hour. Up against two provinces, the two most considerable in the country, it would have been still harder, if not downright impossible, for Ottawa to rectify the 1964 'error' that let Quebec take the option to contract out.

The dossier on contracting out from shared cost programs prompts a few observations at this point. First, Quebec extracted no new power from the operation and moreover failed to limit that of the federal government. Quebec did not achieve total responsibility for any new area, since the transition period provided for extension of the status quo. (Had this period ended on the date set, this point would obviously lose a great deal of its appositeness.)

All the programs for which Quebec won the right to collect 20 additional tax points instead of getting federal subsidies fell within provincial jurisdiction and had already been subject to numerous federal intrusions. In opting out of them — even if its room for manoeuvre had been unlimited, which certainly was not the case — Quebec was simply repossessing some of its own territory. The federal decision to allow contracting out was actually in part a response to some venerable Quebec claims, refurbished by Jean Lesage at the beginning of the Quiet Revolution.

The programs subject to the option were all 'established' programs. The title of the federal Act is revealing: Law on Established Programs (Interim Arrangements). In its initial position Quebec itself had suggested that the right of contracting out be applied to this type of program. Later, however, Ottawa fastened itself unremittingly on the position that served its own purpose, knowing perfectly well that even if a hypothetical deadline were set, few provinces would run the political risk of cancelling or profoundly modifying the established programs.

At the same time Ottawa took great care not to expose such programs as those involving research and experimentation. The argument then advanced for withholding them was based on the impossibility of forward cost accounting; the real federal motive, however, was connected with the very nature of these programs, which fostered new activity in unexplored areas, giving Ottawa a chance to dream up fresh schemes for poaching in the provincial preserves. 'Experimental' interference thus remained possible in education, for example, or municipal affairs. Frequently, the results of such experiments would whet the provinces' appetites for increased or permanent federal participation: hence, a new shared program. The government in Ottawa held on to its potential leadership in cases of obvious 'national need.'

Even though there was agreement in principle that the status quo would be respected during the transition period, Ottawa went ahead to propose certain changes for programs in force. To the extent that modification won acceptance on both sides there was nothing wrong with this. One major alteration, however, was the subject of a unilateral federal government decision. The public health program, for which Quebec had obtained one tax point, was cancelled in 1967. Although provinces objected to the spiriting away of the subsidies, Ottawa stuck to its guns. As a consequence Quebec lost the relevant tax point; the total fiscal equivalence accompanying withdrawal from the shared cost programs dropped from 20 points to 19.

It matters little whether or not the reasons Ottawa advanced for cancelling the health grants were valid. What we have to learn from the experience is that there is no guarantee that the points now held as fiscal equivalence will be Quebec's indefinitely. The longer transition is dragged out, the greater the danger that Ottawa may cancel other shared programs by ceasing for one reason or another to participate in them financially. Ottawa would thus do away with the basis of the fiscal abatements given Quebec at the time of withdrawal. By means of a constantly-extended period of transition Ottawa can also profoundly alter its mode of contribution to the financing of these programs, or even the amount of the contribution. In either case the tax points now held by Quebec would be affected.

Ottawa's attitude on continual extension of the transition period can be explained only by eager anticipation of a political juncture where the state of Quebec-Ottawa relations favours 'normalization' of Quebec in this particular domain. The most Ottawa can do at present is, under duress, tolerate its participation in shared cost programs taking the form of a conditional fiscal abatement — conditional in the sense that the programs are still subject to federal regulation. Such is Quebec's present situation. For Ottawa, in any case, the happiest eventuality would be the disappearance of the fiscal equivalence itself and its replacement by financial contributions of the same type as those awarded to provinces that did not take advantage of the contracting-out option in 1964. This would put us back in the old state of affairs, and Quebec would have lost an element of its originality. This hope is naturally not about to be crowned. Although it may sometimes be erratic in terms of complete takeover of the shared cost programs, the Quebec government is perfectly well aware of the political dangers that lurk in retrocession of the tax points acquired amid such rejoicing in 1964.

The tendency to protect federal prerogatives in shared cost programs cannot be laid solely at the door of frustrated obstinacy. The stakes are substantial, in fact. In 1964, very few federal representatives had weighed the real impact of the withdrawal option on the working of the Canadian federal system. The main point then was to locate short-term relief for a high-tension situation by reacting to one of Quebec's demands. As time passed, however, and the expiry date drew near, Ottawa recognized the danger of getting caught up in a sort of politico-administrative mill that might profoundly alter the nature of Quebec's relation to the central government, and hence Quebec's position with respect to Canada as a whole. Quebec might further particularize itself, and by the force of circumstance acquire a distinct system, one result of which would be the reduction of the federal hold on important policies affecting Quebec's population. In consequence of this, as has often been pointed out, the role of federal members from Quebec would be different from that of MPs from the other provinces, and the influence of some federal officials slashed; Quebec would be enjoying a special fiscal deal, and above all the growth of Quebec's freedom to act might, in accordance with the principle that appetite grows with eating, produce further demands in the autonomist vein.

Contemplating such possibilities, looming as they did in the light of the thinking that surrounded constitutional review, Ottawa had not much choice: unless it gave up the virtually unrestrained exercise of its spending power, and lost an important lever for intervention in matters affecting the 'national interest,' unless, in short, it abandoned certain of the powers it had used freely up to that time, Ottawa had to alter the course on which it had allowed itself to be set in 1964. In theory Ottawa could have chosen another policy, as constitutional review favoured it: it could certainly have changed its notion of the role it had been playing up to that time, or again could have taken a fresh view of Quebec. Yet Ottawa consecrated itself to its mission as 'national' government, arguing the need for a strong central power by the exigencies of modern living and the unity of Canada. After this, final withdrawal from the shared cost programs by any province would look like an assault on the newly-defined federal prerogative.

I must emphasize in conclusion that Ottawa had to lighten ballast anyway as far as future shared programs were concerned. Wise after the experience of recent years, and also to take into account doubts provinces sometimes raised on the expediency of a given program at a given time, Ottawa suggested inserting certain rules in the constitution to govern future shared cost programs affecting areas of exclusive provincial jurisdiction. In a White Paper entitled *Federal-Provincial Grants and the Spending Power of Parliament* Ottawa proposed that henceforth such programs be set up only after general agreement by the provinces. At the same time, a province not wishing to take part in any such program would not be penalized. In this case its citizens would receive compensation direct from the federal government, the total for their province equalling the amount that would have been paid out as the Ottawa contribution to the program. Here I may pause to observe that taxpayers in the non-participating province would have paid the federal tax for the new program in any case, whether their province abstained from it or not. Moreover, the compensation an individual received would not necessarily equal the tax he had paid. The result would thus have been a redistribution among the citizens, its scale depending on the type of taxation and rebate.

The federal proposal was a clever one. With compensation flowing back into individual pockets, provincial governments could not use abstention as a way of getting money for their own unrestricted use. Of course they could have gone straight ahead to confiscate individual compensation by enlarged provincial taxes, but the repugnant character of that stratagem is too obvious to require comment: it could have been enough by itself to propel a province into new shared programs. We must also see the federal suggestion of direct reimbursement as a device to allow Ottawa to remain in direct and even 'intimate' contact with the citizen.

The suspension of constitutional review in June 1971 left the federal proposal at the drafting stage. The moment the idea was made known, almost all provinces had risen in opposition to it. They feared the probable administrative complexity of the repayment arrangements as much as the loss of revenue which, in their view, ought to go back to the governments.

Since the right of abstention would have been accepted constitutionally —
and, remember, the shared cost programs in question would have affected areas
of exclusive provincial jurisdiction — provinces would have preferred pure and
simple compensation between governments, or else non-collection of federal
taxes in an amount equal to the cost of the new programs. Logic and politics,
however, are not always congenial bedfellows.

4
Give Us Our Treasure: Fiscal Sharing

A number of people see inadequate distribution of revenue sources among governments as the greatest problem of Canadian federalism. By the same token, they believe, solve this one and virtually all our difficulties are removed.

The opinion is so widely held that for a long time federal-provincial conferences were taken as synonymous with fiscal meetings. In the English-speaking provinces the fiscal issue commanded more attention than any other, and its presence is felt in practically all the criticism they have levelled, not at the federal system itself, of course, but its operation. This same fiscal problem called up a great many flamboyant pronouncements from Maurice Duplessis, who considered Quebec pillaged of its 'spoils' in the fiscal arrangements agreed to during the Second World War by Adélard Godbout.

The fiscal or financial distribution among the governments has always been the principal ingredient of any provincial 'common front.' Whenever there was a chance to raise the question the provinces have jumped at it. It became as it continued to be a sort of *leitmotiv* of federal-provincial relations.

In an Ottawa conference during July 1960 Jean Lesage called for a fiscal abatement in favour of Quebec — and the other provinces as well — equal to 25 per cent of the federal tax on personal income, 25 per cent of the federal tax on corporate income, and 100 per cent of inheritance tax: the 25-25-100 formula. Lesage returned to the charge in various speeches, notably his presentation of the Quebec budget on 5 April 1963, during which he flung out what was then regarded as an ultimatum. It was only three days before a federal election when the Quebec premier used these words: 'Twelve months will go by before the next budget speech. Either the federal government, whatever party is elected on April 8, and I repeat, whatever the party elected on April 8, the central government will have made use of the 12 months to make allowance for Quebec's needs or else we in Quebec will have taken steps on our own side to make the required decisions in fiscal policy. And the decisions will be those imposed on us by the aims of economic, social, and cultural affirmation we have set ourselves at the request of the people of Quebec!'

The spectre of 'double taxation' was abroad. There was a certain historical significance in the Lesage ultimatum; Quebec had not struck such an aggressive pose since the day of the tax levied by Duplessis in 1954. Fiscal sharing took place of honour in the agenda for the federal-provincial conference of March and April 1964. It was also featured in the 'package deal' that emerged in the wake of the conference, amid the tensions that event generated, and which included as well, as we have seen, the Quebec Pension Plan and, some months later, Quebec's opting out of the shared cost programs.

By the terms of the 1962-7 fiscal arrangements the provinces would receive, either by direct collection or by way of Ottawa, 16 per cent of personal income tax in 1962, 17 per cent in 1963, 18 per cent in 1964, 19 per cent in 1965, and 20 per cent in 1966. This was the arrangement challenged in the spring of 1964. Ottawa leapt instantly to the defence of the existing distribution pattern, but did suggest the striking of a committee on the tax structure to conduct a comparative depth study of the revenues and expenditures of all governments in Canada. Quebec refused to have its finance minister sit on this committee without an improvement in revenue sharing, and in April 1964 this improvement finally came: wishing to resolve the pension dilemma, anxious to repair the resounding failure of the conference, and confronted with the assembled force of all the provincial governments, the federal government agreed to raise the provincial share of personal income tax by two points for 1965 and four for 1966. This would give provinces 21 points instead of 19 the following year, and 24 instead of 20 the next. Here again, though in a less sonorous register, was a victory for co-operative federalism.

This supplementary abatement of 1964 is read as victory if one starts from the principle that in Canada the normal tax collector is the federal administration, which can condescend or not, according to the circumstances, to be open-handed to the lesser administrations of the provinces. In the logic of that revelation of Canada's political structure, one with relatively few subscribers in Quebec but propitiated elsewhere, the 1964 arrangements evidenced the broad understanding spirit of the Canadian government and merited an unequivocal vote of thanks from provinces that seemed permanently discontented with their lot.

In the view of any reasonable person who does not embrace the federal monopoly over the country's fiscal resources as an article of faith, these 1964 arrangements appear as at most a rectification of an unjust distribution of tax revenue, given foreseeable needs in both orders of government. It was already recognized at the time that the provinces' needs in their jurisdictions — education, health, welfare, etc. — were outstripping their fiscal resources, and that the situation was getting worse. Mr Lesage referred to the provinces' 'priority needs' in an attempt to highlight their greater significance as against 'needs' that were merely possible on the part of the federal régime. Ottawa's situation was not necessarily one of abundance, but it was admitted that the financial balance of that administration was not and was unlikely to become as risky as the provinces'.

These impressions, buttressed by figures as precise as they could be at the time, were later confirmed by the highly elaborate technical studies of the Tax Structure Committee. Made public in 1966, its report showed with supporting figures that while provinces were moving towards such deficits as daunted the imagination, Ottawa, with the potential aid of the Bank of Canada, would be more or less able to squeak by. The average annual increase in provincial and municipal spending was forecast at 8.5 per cent for the period 1967-72, compared to 6.5 per cent for the expenditure of the federal government. Since that time, in fact, provincial deficits have mounted as foreseen, though Ottawa's potential surplus has not been realized as the federal authorities became involved in such costly new services as medicare.

From today's standpoint we find it hard to imagine how, in 1964, the central government could have continued to withhold the required readjustment. It might have been put off for a year, or even two, but against pressure from all the provinces Ottawa would soon have found it impossible to carry on. A similar reasoning may be applied to the improved equalization of the same year. There are no grounds for reading Ottawa's decision to improve the sharing of resources as one of those historic shifts that sometimes characterize political systems in rapid evolution, especially since this was the last improvement in fiscal sharing and in fact the only one between 1960 and 1971, even taking into account the better equalization formula first used in 1966.

The 1964 fiscal transfer prompted no federal 'reconquest' attempt that could be compared with that over the Quebec Pension Plan or the withdrawal from shared cost programs. The transfer was accessible to all provinces, and not only Quebec, just as the 1966 improvements in equalization affected all provinces eligible to benefit from them. This type of federal-provincial progress differs from those gains that have the effect of underlining Quebec's particularism. Here, the federal posture is unchanged with regard to any specific province. For this reason Ottawa might think it less urgent to repair the damage later on. The Canadian political balance is less sensitive to its effects.

Certainly more sensitive is the field of education, in which Quebec set up a pioneer schooling allowances program in 1961 aimed at young people of 16 and

17. Allowances were to encourage continued attendance, a condition of the benefit. In 1964, however, the federal government announced a plan to set up an identical program across Canada, including, of course, Quebec. Ottawa took it for granted that the Quebec government would retire from the field and find other uses for the money saved by cancelling the provincial program. Quebec wanted to keep up its own allowances, however, for this area fell squarely within provincial jurisdiction, and instead asked Ottawa not to take the program into Quebec but pay as a supplementary fiscal abatement the funds that would have been allocated for it. Finally Quebec's position was accepted, and a special abatement of three percentage points of personal income tax put through.

Ottawa's gesture was hedged about with reservations, and these were only heightened by the obvious fact that the concession was valid for Quebec alone. Seven watchful years later, in the fall of 1971, Ottawa glimpsed a possibility of rescuing the three stranded points. The move was made at a propitious moment in Quebec-Ottawa talks on family allowances.

As no agreement had been reached at the Victoria constitutional conference on a text clearly laying down provincial paramountcy in social affairs, discussions then began between Ottawa and Quebec to see whether, in the absence of any constitutional amendment acceptable to both parties, some administrative arrangement could be found that would allow Ottawa to maintain a federal family allowance program while Quebec decided how the program was to operate in its own territory. Quebec had in fact put forward some fairly specific suggestions regarding family allowances, first in January 1966 in the Quebec brief to the federal-provincial conference on the Canada Assistance Plan, then in January 1967 in its brief to the conference of social welfare ministers, and again on several occasions after that. Moreover, Quebec had created its own system of family allowances in 1967, run on a progressive scale according to the number and order of children in a family. Following the 1971 Castonguay-Nepveu Commission report, Quebec projected an exhaustive family allowance program in which a selective system would take the place of the federal system then in force. All these proposals were moving in the same direction, and in the end strongly influenced Ottawa, which after careful examination drew inspiration from them to effect changes in its own family allowance program.

In 1972, Quebec-Ottawa discussions dragged on, producing contradictory statements from the prime ministers of Quebec and Canada. It was hoped to reach an arrangement that would give Quebec some latitude, and on 13 March 1972, the Canadian prime minister revealed an offer he had just sent to Quebec City, outlining a scheme by which Quebec would enjoy more freedom to work out its income security policy within minimal federal norms, but which fell far short of the aims expressed by Quebec in earlier policy statements on the subject. In any event there was no longer any question of recognizing the legislative paramountcy Quebec wanted in the area.

One of the features of the new Ottawa family allowance scheme was its extension to the 16- and 17-year-olds. In negotiations preceding Ottawa's March proposal Quebec imagined that, given an acceptable arrangement with Ottawa, all youth allowances could be administered directly by the federal authorities under Quebec supervision. For reasons of administrative convenience, in other words, Quebec intended to delegate the operation of the youth allowance program that had yielded three points of personal income tax since 1964. The move backfired: though Quebec had never dreamed of shedding the three points, the mere suggestion of delegating operation to Ottawa afforded the federal people an opening to raise the issue of the special abatement. Since federal thinking excluded the idea of Quebec's own program for 16- and 17-year-olds continuing, it followed automatically that the abatement relating to the program should go up in smoke. In rebutting this argument Quebec claimed that it wanted to keep control of its own youth allowance program except that, to simplify administration, it had had the idea of trusting Ottawa with the cheque-mailing job, and no more.

When the prime minister of Canada sent Quebec his offer the 'misunderstanding' had been cleared up. For this reason the federal proposal stipulated that Quebec would retain the three tax points, but that the province would deliver the product to Ottawa. However, this gesture must not be allowed to obscure the fact that there was an attempt by Ottawa to get the points back.

It may be wondered why the cession or retention of a tax point here and there can arouse such feeling. There is a fairly widespread impression, confirmed in a sense by the deductions noted on pay slips, that with time and intense bargaining Quebec managed to get free hold of half the taxes, whereas such was far from the case ten or twenty years ago. We must examine this impression closely. It has often been a basis for wrong thinking, notably that Quebec now has unconditional possession of a vastly more extensive fiscal ground.

The 1972 *Quebec Yearbook* indicates the number of tax points conceded by the federal government in the period 1957-71. With the total of personal income and inheritance taxes represented by a basis of 100 points apiece, Quebec, receiving only ten per cent of personal income tax in 1957, controlled 50 per cent in 1971. For inheritance tax, Quebec's percentage rose in the same period from 50 to 75. One might point out that the yield of this tax for Quebec is little more than one-tenth that of the provincial abatement on income tax, to which I will soon return.

As regards the tax on corporate income, its yield for Quebec was approximately half that of the personal income tax. The base total for this tax is

50 points, as in the case of the personal income tax and the inheritance tax. This means that in 1971, with ten points out of a total of 50, Quebec really received 20 per cent of corporate income tax. From 1960 to 1966 inclusive one of those ten points is distinguished in the breakdown given in the *Yearbook*: this is the fiscal equivalence granted Quebec to replace federal grants to universities after the Sauvé-Barrette-Diefenbaker arrangements of 1959-60. Beginning in 1967, Ottawa granted an unconditional fiscal abatement amounting to one point of corporation tax and four of personal income tax to allow the provinces to better meet increasing costs in post-secondary education. For this reason the abatement on corporation tax since 1967 is listed as ten points and not as nine plus one.

Returning to the personal income tax abatement, the most important of the three, Quebec's unconditional share of that tax seems to have risen from ten to 50 per cent. This is by no means the case. Taking 1971 as an example, the 50 points are divided as follows: 28 points of general abatement accessible to all provinces, three points granted Quebec in compensation for its youth allowance program, and 19 representing the fiscal equivalence relating to Quebec's withdrawal from shared cost programs — this equivalence previously amounted to 20 points, but was reduced in 1967 after Ottawa cancelled the public health grants. The three youth allowance points and the 19 shared cost program points are conditionally abated, representing part of the Ottawa contribution to specific programs that cannot be cut out or radically changed without the abatement itself being jeopardized. Of the 28 points remaining, four were conceded in 1967 in replacement of a substantial portion of federal aid to higher education. Twenty-four thus remain as authentically unconditional: in return for these Quebec is not obliged to absorb expenditures paid previously by Ottawa. If we want an accurate picture of Quebec's advance in terms of 'net fiscal reconquest' it is these 24 points, available moreover to any province, that we must set beside the ten of 1957, the 13 of 1960, the 16 of 1962, and the 17 of 1963.

Are we entitled to conclude that Quebec has at its unconditional command 24 per cent of all federal income taxes relative to its population? No, for there are in reality federal taxes on personal income that do not enter into the 100 base points. This was the case with the Social Development Tax and also with the former Old Age Security Tax. Taking this factor into consideration and adding in the mass of personal taxes with the surtaxes Quebec occasionally levies itself, we find that the government of Quebec can freely spend less than 20 per cent of the total tax on personal income paid by the people of the province. We are far from that vaunted 50 per cent.

From 1972 on, following the Ottawa fiscal reforms, the system of tax abatement outlined here has been continued in the case of corporation taxes, but abolished in that of personal income tax. Previously, as noted above, we had been expressing the personal income tax of the province as a percentage of a basic federal tax before abatement, with the federal tax corresponding to 100 per cent. The basic tax was taken as a fixed starting point from which one went on to establish the province's share. From now on, however, the provincial tax would be expressed as a percentage of the Ottawa tax 'payable', a change that means there is no longer, as there was before, one federal tax with one product to be shared between Ottawa and the province. Inheritance taxes had been abolished already by the federal government in fiscal reform. None of these changes, however, affects the general bearing of the analysis offered here.

It is worth inquiring whether the benefits of equalization are any more real. Certainly, since the machinery was set up in 1957, a number of changes have been made in the formula for calculating equalization. Just as certainly, Quebec has reaped some notable financial benefits, as have all provinces whose relative poverty places them in the way of this type of payment. All these advantages appear to be permanent, and so far we have seen no federal recovery operation in their honour. Up to now they have not affected the provinces' political status, and the standards are applied automatically to each.

In discussing equalization, however, we generally omit to take note of certain useful details. For instance, there is a tendency to view the redistribution of resources as a proof of enlightened federal generosity, as if the central government were doing without its own income in order to rain benefits on the poorer provinces. Certainly the tax man feeding the equalization mill is the federal one, and in that sense he performs a service for the recipient provinces when he consents to tax for this purpose. However, the financial resources he redistributes come, in the final reckoning, from the citizens of all Canada. We may also presume that if equalization did not exist, a portion of the fiscal burden imposed on us all by Ottawa would also lose its basis, which amounts to saying that equalization causes the federal government no hardship at all. For a recipient province, moreover, equalization does not constitute a net profit. Quebec, for example, which now receives approximately $650 million a year in equalization, still has to pay the federal taxes included in the amount coming back. As about one quarter of Ottawa's revenue originates in Quebec, this means that Quebec contributes 25 per cent of the total amount Ottawa sets aside for equalization, or 25 per cent of $1.4 billion ($350 million). Quebec's 'net profit' in equalization is thus $300 ($650 less $350) million.

Does this mean that Quebec's adherence to the federation 'pays' us around $300 million net a year? Not at all, for if we want a true estimate of the financial advantages Confederation brings Quebec, we have to take into account a fairly complex and interrelated body of data of all kinds. We must certainly total up all federal payments, not only those made under equalization, and compare them to the portion of Ottawa's revenue originating in Quebec. It is no small task, but it has been done by the Quebec department of Intergovernmental Affairs in a study that was issued soon after the 1970 election: *La Part du Québec dans les dépenses et les revenus du gouvernement fédéral de 1960-61 à 1967-68*. There is nothing more recent on the subject. Still, it is interesting to recall the main conclusions: they throw valuable light on Quebec gains of recent years in the financial sphere. According to the study: 'From 1960-61 to 1967-68 Quebec gained no more from federal expenditures made on its behalf than it contributed to them. More specifically, it received from the federal government only those benefits for which it paid, and derived no benefit greater than its own contribution.' The same document adds: 'In a sense, through the revenue its citizens and institutions pay to the federal government, Quebec funds its own equalization.'

5
The Urban Guerrilla: Housing and Renewal

In 1967, as proposed by an ad hoc committee of federal and provincial officials, agreement was reached between Ottawa and Quebec City on administering sums paid out for public housing and urban renewal through the federal Central Mortgage and Housing Corporation. By the terms of this agreement the Quebec Housing Corporation, a new provincial body charged with promoting renewal of housing stock as well as new building, and also helping to ensure accessibility for Quebec citizens at moderate cost, assumed full responsibility for preparing and implementing these programs of upgrading and construction, a responsibility that included locating and planning the projects as well as finding personnel to carry them out. From now on, Quebec project submissions would go to the CMHC solely for a decision on their eligibility for federal loans or subsidies.

This agreement dramatically enhanced the Quebec Housing Corporation's role and by the same stroke reduced the federal corporation to a straightforward purveyor of funds. One of Quebec's aims at the time was direct involvement in the important area of urban renewal and, from there, the whole business of city planning and development — or, perhaps more accurately, forestalling federal involvement in the field. One of the tools Quebec relied on in the venture was its housing corporation.

The federal government's main short-term concern was to show that Quebec could begin benefiting from impressive sums for public housing and urban renewal, sums claimed already by certain provinces and in particular by Ontario, where a provincial housing corporation had been in operation for some time. The gap between federal payments to Ontario and those Quebec had been able to get was such that it was important, in order to dodge criticism, to correct the imbalance as swiftly as possible. Since 1954, in fact, Ontario had received approximately 50 per cent and Quebec only 20 per cent of amounts loaned or guaranteed by Ottawa for home construction. The Quebec Housing Corporation looked as if it was equipped to pinpoint the targets for federal aid, and so Ottawa consented to use it.

This particular Quebec-Ottawa agreement went virtually unnoticed at the time. It did not produce the usual declarations of mutual triumph and seemed nothing more than an unspectacular administrative reshuffle. At least that was how the federal people saw it. For Quebec its significance was vastly greater, and looked forward to a dynamic role for the Housing Corporation that would justify its creation. It dawned on the federal government only later that danger lurked in this new formula for the discretionary exercise of the powers it wanted in urban affairs.

The federal government has always carefully emphasized its intention of getting directly into the municipal affairs field at some point. Its entry has been gradual, however. First, Ottawa enlarged the CMHC's responsibilities in urban renewal. Then it took advantage of the facts that harbours, airports, and railways fell within its jurisdiction and it held real estate and installations in all the larger communities in the country to get closely involved in urban planning. The interest was expressed initially in contacts with municipal officials on questions of current administration. The proposal for a more organized relation between Ottawa and the municipalities came later. For Ottawa the problems of urban concentration, transport, deterioration in the centres of certain cities, and so on, have also become issues of 'national interest' in the last few years. On this point Ottawa's statements at the time of the federal-provincial housing conference in December 1967 were sufficiently clear.

At the end of 1970 came the announcement of the creation of a new federal department of State for Urban Affairs and Housing. The rhetorical precautions cloaking this move were truly typical. It was stoutly maintained on the one hand that the federal government's main intention was to co-ordinate activity in the urban field then emanating from the various federal departments concerned with housing, harbours, federal properties, and so on. Since Ottawa controlled real estate in cities, in other words, it should get interested in the cities themselves. Commenting on the throne speech in which the new department was announced, Mr Robert Andras, the future ministerial incumbent, remarked on 8 October 1970: 'The federal government today recognizes in a concrete way that it is deeply involved, in myriad but often unco-ordinated ways, in the problems of Canadian cities already; it recognizes that it must transform that involvement in much more integrated ways.' On the other hand Ottawa rushed out with the statement that the new department must also, in close co-operation with the provinces and of course without infringing on provincial rights, 'set national objectives.' To give it an effective arm, it would be given responsibility for the CMHC along with the corporation's urban renewal and housing programs.

Quebec had always been distinctly touchy when it thought it saw Ottawa meddling in the municipal sector. One has lost count of ministerial statements in this vein. Nonetheless, early in the summer of 1970 Maurice Tessier, the new Quebec minister of municipal affairs, told a Halifax meeting that he personally did not see why the municipalities could not establish their own lines of communication with Ottawa. Back in Quebec City he had to 'clarify' his thinking in response to questions from members of the National Assembly. Still, as one might say, the damage was done. In the other provinces, as among municipal officials desirous of direct federal involvement, it was taken as established that from then on Quebec would put no obstacle in the way of federal-municipal relations. It was the first time they had heard a Quebec minister speak this way. Instantly recast or not, Tessier's statement stood in glaring contrast to those of his predecessors.

Ontario had never been especially enthusiastic at the prospect of federal intervention in municipal affairs. Its stand had often been close to Quebec's, though determined by administrative considerations, while Quebec was also invoking its responsibilities under the constitution. Other provinces, however, were much less reserved about direct channels between Ottawa and their municipalities. Since the federal government had abundant cash resources from which they knew they could benefit on the rebound, the other provinces, and in fact Ontario too most of the time, always came to at least a tacit acceptance of Ottawa's municipal largesse. As for the municipal officials, the vast majority, excepting a certain number of Quebec mayors, were forever clamouring for a concrete demonstration of federal concern with the cities and their problems. In other words, sensing the potential of added financial assistance from Ottawa, they had long wanted the central government to overcome its constitutional misgivings and steam stoutheartedly into municipal waters.

Curiously enough, it took the federal government a good deal of time to make up its mind to such a breakthrough. Quebec's negative attitude may have been somewhat discouraging. More probably the sheer immensity of municipal needs proved daunting financially. In any event Ottawa's move was some time coming. One federal minister, Paul Hellyer, resigned his portfolio partly because Ottawa would not, contrary to his recommendations, get massively involved in the urban sector.

By 1970 federal hesitation had evaporated, and the question was now not whether Ottawa would increase its involvement but precisely how it would do so. It had realized that the urban environment would rank as one of the main concerns facing government from now to the end of this century. Ottawa stuck to certain forms, at least: as we have seen, it was always insured against accusations of invading a provincial jurisdiction. We were even privileged to attend the birth of a new idea: the distinction between 'municipal affairs' and 'urban problems.' The former, Ottawa conceded, were not strictly its affair. It could not, however, remain indifferent to the latter.

The ministry of State for Urban Affairs and Housing, that child of a lengthy pilgrimage across the 'grey areas' of the BNA Act, emerged in this atmosphere. Behind statements of intention draped hastily with the remaining tatters of their political modesty, the federal authorities were assuming a major responsibility in urban affairs. In Ottawa's view, the assumption of leadership should be accompanied by specific policies calling for provincial participation. Accordingly there were repeated appeals for co-operation in the face of the common 'national' problem of urban sprawl and its consequences. But vehicles were also needed for the federal spending power to operate freely. The CMHC was obviously to be one of them.

In setting up its new ministry, Ottawa had not failed to notice that the 1967 agreement with Quebec, renewed annually since that time, could turn out to be an obstacle. Moreover, other provinces were likely to claim agreements similar to Quebec's. Toronto was showing interest in enlarging the activities of the Ontario Housing Corporation. Undoubtedly Ottawa owed it to itself to modify the scope of the Quebec accord. It must make use of the annual renegotiation ceremony to challenge, in as veiled a manner as possible, the role of the Quebec Housing Corporation, hoping to transfer its main functions to the federal body. During the renegotiation of the agreement for 1970-71, when federal aims had been fully defined, this challenge was introduced.

The 1969 agreement fell due on 1 April 1970. Renegotiation did not open until the summer, having been somewhat delayed by the change of government in Quebec City. From the very beginning the agreement had included the following paragraph (number 6 in section 3) defining the Quebec Housing Corporation's role and by the same token limiting that of the CMHC: 'It is agreed by the parties that the statement of admissibility has as its sole purpose to determine whether the project can be liable for a loan under the Act and to fix the amount of that loan; the Quebec Housing Corporation has sole responsibility for evaluating the need, deciding the site and numbers as well as the extent of the housing, for approving the planning, architecture, plans and estimates, norms and conditions of occupancy; and no certificate of admissibility will be refused or delayed for considerations based on these subjects or others of the same nature.' In other words the Quebec corporation would decide what housing projects could be eligible for federal aid, and determine every aspect of the project other than financial. When it was ready it would call on its banker, the CMHC, to make the decision on funding.

The federal minister responsible for the CMHC in 1967 was well aware of the significance of this arrangement, since in an 18 July letter of that year he informed his Quebec opposite number that the responsibility for preparing and implementing the relevant programs belonged to Quebec. In his response of 12 September the Quebec minister, after a general description of the Quebec Housing Corporation's function, went into detail using virtually the same words: a submission to the CMHC would have as its sole purpose the decision on the Quebec project's admissibility for a loan or grant. It was all quite clear to both parties at the time.

This did not stop the federal representatives at the 1970 renegotiation from stating that it had never been clearly established that the functions of the federal corporation were to be as limited as the Quebeckers liked to think. In any case, they went on, clarification of the passage cited was needed to avoid 'later misunderstanding.' They suggested the addition of this short paragraph: 'It is agreed that the provisions of the present paragraph 6 be subject to examination between now and April 1, 1971.' As Quebec's representatives knew perfectly well that any 'examination' of the passage would leave the door wide open for a challenge to the 1967 arrangement, they refused. On 25 November 1970, the issue was laid before the Cabinet in Quebec City, which resolved by order-in-council to strike out the paragraph Ottawa proposed. The federal negotiators then insinuated that in the face of this attitude, federal generosity in urban renewal and housing programs might well recede. Indeed it was far from impossible, in their view, that the agreement itself might fail to be renewed. More intense discussion ensued and it was at last agreed, in December 1970, to strike out the paragraph, with a new article added to provide for a bilateral committee 'to better define the modes of co-operation between the (federal) Corporation and the Quebec Corporation under the terms of the said convention.' The article stipulated also that the committee must conclude its work before 'the signing of any similar subsequent convention.'

Shortly after this, the 1970-1 agreement was signed. Time was the essential gain, as the solution of the problem was deferred until the next renegotiation. Since the new article had to do with the 'modes of co-operation' and not now with a specific passage in the agreement, Quebec's representatives hoped to make use of the widening of discussion to secure new advantages they had not demanded back in 1967. Ottawa, for its part, had by no means abandoned hope of restricting the freedom Quebec had obtained in 1967. Everyone was pleased.

The agreement was renewed, and a committee on 'mechanisms and procedures' was appointed in 1972. The committee was more or less active, with the nub of the issue left in suspense, partly by mutual consent and partly because the existing situation still made it possible for Ottawa and Quebec City to maintain their respective positions in every detail. Subsequent agreements were signed on virtually the same conditions as the 1970-1 one as regards the CMHC's role. In the 1974 legislative session the Quebec government further defined the powers of its own housing corporation, in part to improve its stance against federal ambition. At the time of writing, nothing in this area has been settled conclusively. Quebec has not lost hope completely. Ottawa certainly has not.

6
Special Friendships: France and Quebec

The unprecedented happened in Canada during February 1965. A province of Confederation — Quebec, as you might expect — concluded an agreement with a foreign nation. The foreign nation was France. The agreement covered a program of educational exchange and co-operation.

An exchange agreement had already been signed in 1964 between the Youth Minister of Quebec and the ASTEF — Association pour l'organisation des stages en France, since metamorphosed into the ACTIM, the Agence pour la co-opération technique, industrielle et économique. (This agreement was an administrative one, however, lacking the formal character of the new accord.) There was more to come: that November, France and Quebec signed again, this time in the area of cultural exchange. Both cases attracted wide publicity. The innovative quality of the agreements was strongly emphasized by Quebec. Ottawa maintained a prudent and discreet stance, yet took pains to minimize the events' significance.

For they were indeed innovative, even though in the circumstances they were qualified by the neutral term 'entente.' During Ottawa-Quebec talks preceding the February 1965 signature it was judged that the traditional language of 'convention,' 'accord,' 'treaty,' was all too meaningful in international usage. Quebec was concerned at the same time to stress the importance and scope of these ententes, and accordingly on each occasion the provincial cabinet passed special orders-in-council authorizing their official signature. Later, when some tried to make over-stringent use of the ententes as evidence of the 'special' behaviour of Quebec, 'not a province like the others,' or else to claim with unnecessary clarity that Quebec had managed to get into new domains despite federal obstruction, appeal was made to multifarious 'precedents' involving other provinces, particularly Ontario. A federal White Paper entitled *Federalism and International Relations* made much of ties other provinces had managed to establish with foreign countries. This was all intended to reduce the impact of the France-Quebec ententes, an attempt that would never enjoy total success because agreements implicating other provinces were really different in kind, being straightforward administrative arrangements between states. The ententes Quebec signed had an 'international' connotation, for they were flanked by political and juridical measures none of the others possessed.

Certainly the federal people displayed no enthusiasm for Quebec's international flings. Nor did Ottawa throw itself firmly in their way, though it did settle down to weigh every word in every phrase of every entente, and lavished a great deal of effort on legitimizing it all through appropriate exchanges of letters or diplomatic notes with Paris. Briefly, Ottawa kept close watch to see that everything was done with its explicit assent, even going so far in November 1965, a week after the France-Quebec cultural entente, as to sign with the French a blanket agreement of its own.

When Ottawa heard talk of a second France-Quebec entente, in fact, it had insisted on the proviso that the agreement be preceded by one between itself and Paris. According to this federal agreement, Canadian provinces would be able to conclude agreements with France so long as they had duly informed the federal authorities and providing the agreements fell into one or another of the categories listed. It was understood at the same time that these agreements involving France with Canadian provinces could be concluded either under the blanket document or by means of an exchange of letters between Paris and Ottawa. In the case of its entente of November 1965, Quebec refused to submit to the federal accord and left it to France and Canada to exchange correspondence.

By general consensus among Ottawa officials, the France-Canada agreement marked a first step in the development of a new concept of international relations and foreign policy. It ought normally to be followed, they said, by other and similar agreements with other countries, especially the homelands of substantial ethnic minorities. It seemed we must expect those provinces inhabited by the minorities to be as keen as Quebec was to forge cultural links. There has been no sequel, as we know, to the agreement between Canada and France. It is obvious now as well that only Quebec has shown interest in international relations, something easily predictable at the outset. We must understand that the federal aim in 1965 was to keep Quebec well under control by locking it into the framework of a general agreement made after the event, and minimize what Quebec was doing by citing past or future acts by other provinces supposedly animated by international concerns which were identical to Quebec's. From this viewpoint Quebec could claim no particularism whatsoever, being only 'a province like the others.'

In ensuing years, amid the growing profusion of France-Quebec exchanges and political ties established between Paris and Quebec City, the federal government found an added reason for not entering into similar agreements. Ottawa preferred to work out an entire doctrine on the unity of the country's presence abroad and set its face like stone against even a hint of international presence in provincial powers.

Did Quebec's signing of the ententes in fact mark any sort of 'gain' over its former position? The answer here is affirmative, but it is essential to note a few significant subtleties. Let us say in the first place that any gain lay chiefly in Quebec's new capability to work out programs of co-operation directly with France, in the absence of federal middlemen. This gain was not a constitutional one, then, nor was it even juridical, according to some federal functionaries: it was administrative in character, as Ottawa had made sure Quebec's signings did not jeopardize the country's position internationally. In the second place, the gain was possible chiefly because it was not appreciated as such by the federal government of the day. Ottawa only realized later that, in its direct relations with France, Quebec was now poised not only to hatch new exchange programs or even simply discuss political problems with French representatives, but also to consult with Paris as if it were a virtually sovereign state and, thanks to French support, be bidden to international gatherings on the same basis as the other nations of the world.

Although originally concerned with exchange programs only, the France-Quebec rapprochement of 1965 moved with time into a more intimate governmental connection. At regular intervals Quebec ministers discussed the exchanges and other joint activities with members of the French cabinet. One after another, Quebec prime ministers themselves were led to meet with French leaders, who in turn found occasion to visit Quebec. Mr Lesage had gone to France for the opening of the Quebec Delegation-General in October 1961. In 1964 he returned, and on this occasion the possibility first arose, between a Quebec premier and a French president, of agreements linking the two states. In September 1966 French foreign minister Couve de Murville came to make contact with the new Quebec administration. Mr Johnson travelled to Paris in May 1967. In July General de Gaulle made his historic voyage to Quebec. In September of the same year he was followed by education minister Alain Peyrefitte, and with authority from De Gaulle the minister worked out details of new exchange programs with his Quebec colleagues in education, Jean-Jacques Bertrand, and cultural affairs, Jean-Noël Tremblay. It was all embodied in a joint communiqué by Messrs Johnson and Peyrefitte.

In September 1968 the French president was represented at Daniel Johnson's funeral by Couve de Murville, now prime minister, along with foreign secretary

De Lipowski, and the two Frenchmen met with the new Quebec premier Jean-Jacques Bertrand. Invited to Paris, Bertrand had to give up the trip because of illness and in January 1969 sent Education Minister Guy Cardinal in his stead. Prime Minister Bourassa's turn to go to France came in April 1971. In February 1972, Claude Castonguay of Social Affairs was on an official Paris visit.

During all this time there were other ministerial contacts with France, too numerous to list here. These meetings, all of them intimately involved with France-Quebec relations, did not pass unnoticed in either Quebec or France. In its role as 'national' government Ottawa took a certain umbrage at this activity, feeling excessively ignored. Approaches in this vein to Paris and Quebec City grew increasingly emphatic. At the time of Bourassa's 1971 French trip Ottawa marshalled a great deal of pressure to ensure that a place was reserved for Canada's ambassador with appropriate protocol at all events in the France-Quebec program. Every time the ambassador was present, Ottawa made sure the fact received publicity. Before the official French visit, Bourassa had gone to Belgium, Britain, West Germany, and Italy; Ottawa's emissaries in all these countries received formal instructions to get themselves seen with the Quebec premier, the ideal being to have their photographs taken in his company.

Given the breadth and political repercussions of these ententes, the Canadian government was finally roused, though at no time did Ottawa directly challenge the new relations. When the trend of France-Quebec contacts seemed to point to diplomatic consequences Ottawa found unacceptable, there was a bout of bad temper that even included talk about a break in relations between Paris and Ottawa, but nothing radical was ever done beyond the occasional dispatch of diplomatic notes intended as friendly reminders to the French of the usages and customs of international protocol as well as the risk it ran, in too pro-Quebec behaviour, of giving offence to the sovereign government of Canada. The most serious clashes occurred at the time of De Gaulle's 1967 visit and in 1969, when France's foreign secretary made statements in Quebec that Ottawa did not take kindly.

What Ottawa did resort to was a campaign, subtler than the call to diplomatic arms, for the 'normalization' of Quebec. The France-Quebec entente called for a 'permanent commission of France-Quebec co-operation' with representatives of both parties, all of them top officials, to meet on an average of twice a year alternately in Quebec City and Paris. The commission would perform a liaison role and oversee the orientation and implementation of the exchange programs. In the long run its importance as an official mechanism of France-Quebec relations grew to be considerable. The terms of the blanket Ottawa-Paris agreement signed in November 1965 called for a similar body, except of course that in this case the French would be meeting nominees of the federal government. The France-Quebec and France-Canada commissions were independent of one another, and in principle did not touch on the same subjects.

Cultural affinity soon made France-Quebec programs much more conspicuous than anything put together between France and the rest of Canada. The mass of exchanges is still accounted for by Quebec, with the result that federal government supervision really covers very little of the activity, an imbalance that has never won favour with the proponents of strict federal control over anything that might resemble 'foreign policy.' Moreover it has all stood as a perennial reminder to France and other interested parties that these exchanges found their substance and meaning in Quebec far more than in the rest of Canada.

Some Ottawa officials had probably suspected that the bulk of France-Quebec relations would dwarf their own, but federal politicians seem not to have realized this until somewhat later. In any event, a scant few months after the signing of the 1965 Ottawa-Paris and Quebec-Paris agreements, federal officials were proposing that the Quebec government appoint people as observers, to attend the commission on France-Canada co-operation where the Canadian representatives were federal. It was not openly stated that a request for reciprocation would follow, so that federal people could observe meetings of the permanent France-Quebec commission, but it was rumoured officially. Some federal people even acknowledged that the aim was an eventual merger of the two bodies, allegedly for reasons of efficiency. The real aim, as will already have been grasped, was to tuck France-Quebec co-operation back into Ottawa's fold.

In 1966 a suggestion for this 'convenient' arrangement reached Mr Lesage. Too well aware of its possible consequences, he turned it down. More formally, this time by letter from the federal minister of external affairs, Daniel Johnson was plied with the identical 'advantage' soon after taking office, and the reply Ottawa received was the same: with the Canadian government's endorsement, the France-Quebec ententes provided for establishing direct ties of co-operation between France and Quebec, and it was important not to disrupt this privileged relation. Jean-Jacques Bertrand was later the recipient of the offer. Then it was Marcel Masse, the intergovernmental affairs minister, then Gérard Lévesque, the Liberal incumbent in the same department, and then, in early 1971, the minister of state at the department. Ottawa's automatic return to the charge has become rather funny: whenever Quebec appoints a new minister of intergovernmental affairs, his officials wait, always with absolute confidence, for the arrival of a federal missive proposing 'close collaboration' between Quebec and Ottawa in France-Quebec relations.

Until now Ottawa's thirst for control over these exchanges has been unassuaged. But perhaps we should rather admire Ottawa's equally great determination and persistence in wanting to reassert a right of endorsement over

Quebec's activities that it considers to be, at most, temporarily in abeyance. The scenario has revenge potential. For some years Quebec had been thinking about a cultural agreement with Belgium, and official talks had even taken place. Then, suddenly, Ottawa told Quebec at the eleventh hour before signing, on 8 May 1967, of a Belgium-Canada cultural accord. This was not a blanket agreement of the previous type. On the evening of 7 May, the prime minister of Quebec replied to his federal opposite number in these words: 'The solemn signing tomorrow without previous consultation of a Belgo-Canadian cultural agreement covering certain areas of our jurisdiction arouses general astonishment here. In consequence we will regretfully be obliged to dissociate ourselves from your action.' Signed anyway, the agreement remains practically sterile for want of Quebec participation.

It has been wondered why, apart from a few verbal outbursts, Ottawa has always limited itself to relatively discreet interference when it was often extremely irritated at the turn France-Quebec affairs were taking, and the tendencies it feared to discern in them. I can offer three complementary explanations for this. The first is that even if Quebeckers have never been especially given to Francophilia, it would have been ill advised from a political standpoint for the federal government to act as if it intended to force an increasingly nationalistic Quebec to withdraw into itself, and curtail the development of its ties with the French-speaking country par excellence, when, moreover, such ties had long been neglected under federal foreign policy. In the second place the federal government had approved the signing of the France-Quebec ententes; Canada was now bound to France by a blanket agreement which allowed Canadian provinces and hence allowed Quebec to maintain direct ties with that nation. It would have been more surprising to see Canada disavow the consequences of its own official acts. Finally, federal ministers and officials have always been persuaded that with General de Gaulle's departure the balance would be restored, and France herself would be urging Quebec to step back quietly into the provincial ranks. That is not now sure, by any means.

7
Liaisons dangereuses:
The International Conferences

Two or three decades ago any orthodox federalist would have been outraged to see a Canadian province as such taking part in an international conference, even if federal representatives were there as well and the conference had to do with subjects that were strictly provincial. The fact is that two or three decades ago the scene of international affairs was not producing today's literal efflorescence of encounters. The problem of provincial attendance at such meetings scarcely arose.

In a more and more interdependent world — a phenomenon that does not run counter, but rather the reverse, to autonomist or regionalist tendencies in various countries like Canada — intergovernmental co-operation and even consultation at the international level have become necessities. For a long time Canada laboured under a handicap in some of its international commitments, owing to the fact that Ottawa lacked power to force compliance on the provinces' part if the issue was one of provincial prerogative. In the White Paper *Federalism and International Relations* this passage is especially enlightening: 'Canada has been placed in an unusual position as compared with other federal states. The federal authorities have the power to enter into treaties but the Parliament of Canada is unable to enact legislation implementing such agreements where the subject matter falls within provincial jurisdiction.'

Given the greater incidence of international gatherings and the variety of subjects coming before them, Canada was more and more at a loss, at least in practical terms, when a position was called for on matters outside its own jurisdiction. How, for example, represented only by its federal government, could Canada go to an international conference to discuss secondary education with authority and credibility? In this and other provincial preserves Ottawa had no claim to be a valid spokesman. The only way out was, according to Ottawa, amendment of the constitution so that the federal authority could force provinces to fulfil its international commitments. Clauses of this kind figure in the constitutions of a number of federal states. It is not hard to predict that it would never win unanimous assent from the provinces, for it would entail the erosion of important areas of provincial power.

By an internal arrangement, even without any such constitutional contrivance, Quebec could trust Ottawa to act as its international spokesman. In other words, after consultation and briefing Ottawa could take the Quebec point of view into account in international conferences, even express it. This pragmatic type of solution, which would have well suited Ottawa, was advanced timidly on occasion by federal representatives. It was never seriously considered in Quebec City. In the long run it would have done injury to the exclusiveness of certain provincial areas, with the federal government eventually using this proxy as a base on which to build new claims — in education, for example. In the Canadian constitutional situation, Quebec's interest in international conferences on education arose from a fundamental, and not merely a formal, problem.

Quebec used this lacuna in the BNA Act when for the first time it was directly invited to take part in such a conference. Besides France, the conference brought together the African and Malagasy French-speaking countries in Libreville, Gabon, in February 1968. Quebec attended on the same footing as the others, all of them sovereign states. Faced with this unprecedented move, executed with French intervention, the federal government vented its indignation by breaking off relations, or more precisely omitting to establish them, with the guilty country. The department of External Affairs had seconded its Yaoundé man to Libreville, but as a March 1968 communiqué revealed: 'In the circumstances the Canadian government considered it appropriate to instruct its ambassador-designate to Gabon not to present his credentials.'

Worried at the risk of repetition, which materialized when Quebec was again invited to Paris the following April for the second conference session, Ottawa launched a broad campaign of 'persuasion' in Quebec City. Prime Minister Pearson, who had already announced his retirement from the political arena, addressed several letters on the subject to Prime Minister Daniel Johnson. These letters were extremely pressing and not without a certain pathos. They are reprinted without Johnson's reply, which arrived too late for inclusion, in the White Paper *Federalism and International Conferences on Education.* Federal pressure was also brought to bear on virtually all the French-speaking African nations. We know now that they were plied with mention of financial and other benefits they could get from Canada if they conformed to more orthodox international practices than the sending of direct invitations to Quebec, a potentially secessionist state in the federation. We may be sure that these nations were edified by sombre delineations of the serious risks they ran, in view of their own internal divisions, by encouraging Quebec's secret separatist fantasies in even a veiled, roundabout way.

In Canada itself the federal authorities decided to mobilize the utmost energy to crack the problem. Quebec's international activity struck Ottawa as utterly intolerable, and liable to give the country an image that could actually do Canada harm in the United Nations or in its foreign relations as a whole. 'The way Quebec is treating us will make us ridiculous on the international scene,' was an expression heard frequently from federal people. Some Quebec politicians found participation in these conferences incongruous themselves, and either refused to understand or else pretended ignorance of the fact that much more was at stake than meaningless niceties of protocol. And the provincial Opposition used the issue to make easy capital at this time.

On the Quebec government side, meanwhile, opinion was still divided. The mass of the population knew little of the issue. For its part, Ottawa perceived the risk clearly — of the seven White Papers on constitutional review two are concerned with foreign relations — and reacted with vigour. Pressure was concentrated on Quebec City, where the prevailing mentality construed all international issues as minor. Quebec had a new prime minister, Jean-Jacques Bertrand, and Ottawa was aware that he was not normally moved to high drama in relations with the outside world. In January 1969 a species of *modus vivendi* began to emerge. Henceforth a Canadian delegation or representation would take part in these conferences and carry a Quebec component with it. Words play an important role here, as Ottawa refused to concede that there could be any Quebec 'delegation' as such. An equivocation of convenience was accepted by both parties. Ottawa would refer to the involvement of a Quebec 'representation' and Quebec, with waning stridency, to a 'delegation.' Sometimes the excursions and stratagems surrounding this episode in Quebec-Ottawa relations seemed closer to political fiction, blackmail, and espionage, even trench warfare.

By common consent the chair of a Canadian delegation was awarded to a Quebec minister. Only Quebec possessed the French-speaking education minister whose presence in the Canadian delegation was required for the federal stratagem to succeed. Quebec's tactical advantage might have been exploited. It was not, for Quebec City was in an accommodating mood. In any event the chairman was a Quebecker, and the problem of double representation from Canada and Quebec was more or less sidestepped. Ambiguity persisted, however, as to Quebec's true status. In practical terms its position and influence often turned out to be decisive. Moreover, Quebec could proclaim its identity with external symbols such as flags as well as through the words of its representatives. I should add at the same time that the 'advantages' accorded to Quebec were extended equally to all such relatively 'French-speaking' provinces as Ontario,

New Brunswick, and Manitoba. Quebec's particularism, although impossible to disguise totally, was by this means made as inconspicuous as possible. The technique became a permanent bit of business in Ottawa's repertoire.

The *modus vivendi* applied to other international occasions having to do, for instance, with the civil service (Lomé, January 1971) and youth and sport (Dakar, in June of the same year). It was employed only for conferences within the world Francophone community, however, and on each occasion the Quebec-Ottawa agreement was ad hoc. Frequent renewal of this ad hoc arrangement nevertheless encourages the belief that it is really a permanent form of international representation, if only for conferences on subjects of clearly provincial jurisdiction within the French-speaking world.

The Agence pour la coopération technique, industrielle et économique (ACTIM) of this French-speaking world was created in Niamey, Niger, in March 1970. Quebec was there amid a representation (or delegation) from Canada. (An initial meeting held in February of the preceding year had laid down the governing principles for such an agency: Quebec had been there as well, as a wing of the Canadian delegation — or representation.) On that first occasion, Quebec, like Ottawa, had its invitation directly from President Hamani Diori, of the Niger republic. In the months following, intense federal activity was concentrated on Niger to forestall the calamity of Quebec's being bidden to the sequel in the same unseemly manner. The African president extricated himself by sending, not a formal invitation, but a letter, in mid-February 1970, informing the premiers of the 'French-speaking' provinces of Canada — Quebec, obviously, but also Ontario, New Brunswick, and Manitoba — that he had asked Ottawa to make up a delegation for the March session. As these same 'French-speaking' provinces had attended the meeting in 1969, the Niger leader ventured to 'presume' that they would again be there in 1970 for the Agency's official birth — a presumption that justified his letter.

In the Ottawa view, Quebec must at no cost be directly invited or even have official contact with the Niger government. An invitation might have served as an argument for Quebec's special character in the French-speaking world, and hence for a special status for the state of Quebec within the Agency. The federal government was aware that Quebec sought such a status and moreover that in this search it was receiving active support from the metropolitan French.

The second Niamey conference in March 1970 was presented with a draft Agency charter. An initial version had been distributed to delegations at the 1969 meeting. Acquainting itself with the document well before the federal people deigned to transmit a copy, the Quebeckers realized that, as it was drawn up, the draft made no provision for a distinct or even formally identified Quebec participation. Their reaction was communicated to Ottawa and also to Paris.

Ottawa stood firm against any accommodation for Quebec, but the French were more understanding. At any rate the problems separating Quebec City and Ottawa on the issue had not been completely ironed out before the second Niamey meeting. After a good deal of behind-the-scenes activity there, however, an extremely important passage was inserted in the charter. It had approval from Canada's federal delegates and satisfied Quebec and everyone else, including, obviously, its chief architects, the French. Paragraph 3 of section 3 of the Agency charter reads as follows: 'In full respect for the sovereignty and international jurisdiction of member states, any government may be admitted as a participating government to the institutions, activities, and programs of the Agency, subject to approval by the member state on whose territory the participating government in question exercises its authority and according to modalities agreed between this government and that of the member state.' In other words, the countries meeting in Niamey were in agreement that Quebec become a participating government, but it was up to Ottawa and Quebec City to reach a prior understanding. As everybody at Niamey was aware, the passage was clearly, although not overtly, focussed on the Quebec case.

Following the change of government in Quebec City the new minister of intergovernmental affairs informed the federal external affairs minister in a letter of 11 June 1970 that it was Quebec's wish to become a 'participating government' in the Agency and requested negotiations for this purpose. A few meetings of federal and provincial people took place early in the fall, but the parleys dragged on. Repeatedly, by word and letter, Quebec's representatives stressed the importance of agreeing on Quebec's status in the Agency. Ottawa seemed in no hurry to resolve the problem. As time passed, however, some sort of resolution became urgent. The next meeting of the Agency was to be held in Canada during October 1971, first in Ottawa and then in Quebec City. Yet it was only in September 1971, just before the conference, that serious discussion recommenced. It had become clear in the interim that Ottawa had not the slightest intention of allowing Quebec any change of status whatever. Federal people had stated in unmistakable terms that Quebec had in a sense always been a 'participating government' through attendance at previous conferences, and that it would be enough simply to entrench the old ad hoc arrangement. For Quebeckers, this interpretation amounted to a denial of the whole import of the passage in the charter dealing with the meaning of 'participating government,' even though the federal people had accepted it in 1970. To this Ottawa retorted that it had never liked the passage, that circumstances and pressure had forced acceptance in Niamey, that if it was all to be done again Ottawa's tack would be different, and so on.

For several months, what was really a double negotiation had been in process between Ottawa and Quebec, as two groups of spokesmen in Quebec City faced a single federal voice. There were on the one hand those who wanted to get the maximum from the charter: whatever anyone said, Ottawa had accepted it. On the other there were those seeking a compromise on the basis not of any progress Quebec could have made with the charter, but of federal concessions they thought possible, which in the event meant very little indeed. The technique of the double negotiation is not a novel one, especially in international questions; it had already and frequently been employed by Ottawa. There had always been conciliatory and understanding people in Quebec City ready to lay the ground for an elegant capitulation even before assessing the possibility of triumph. Ottawa could rely on them, at least to keep shuffling the cards for a while and raise a few hopes.

Beginning in September 1971, Quebec saw a change: the pliable people went to the sidelines for a time, and a somewhat more coherent discussion was possible. The date of the conference was rapidly approaching, and Quebec held a major trump: at the eleventh hour, if it was still unsatisfied with Ottawa's offer, it could always refuse to take part. The federal government would have to admit in front of a number of countries that it was incapable, and on home territory, of persuading a recalcitrant Quebec to take a line more compatible with its own. Moreover, the whole conference plan would be jeopardized, as the second half was set for the Quebec capital. It may be doubted whether, given its fundamentally pacific nature, the Quebec government would have gone so far as to take itself off, but awareness of the availability of this ultimate weapon very likely stiffened its resolve. In addition, Prime Minister Bourassa was determined that Ottawa would sooner or later extend recognition to the 'cultural uniqueness' of Quebec. The Agency conference gave him an excellent chance to demonstrate this unforeseen dimension of the 'paying' quality of federalism. All communications media were alerted, and this put added pressure on Quebec to maintain a reasonably firm stance. Quebec's humiliation in Quebec City itself would be harder to hush up than if it occurred in some distant land.

Right at the beginning of October, less than two weeks before the conference, Quebec and Ottawa found themselves able to agree at last. The Liberal government in Quebec was clearly more anxious to come out of the affair with an absence of losses than additional gains, a mood echoed in the agreement, ratified by exchange of letters between the governments rather than anything more imposing, which assured Quebec a considerable role in Canada's participation in the Agency and its institutions, but no special juridical status as a state. More than anything else it was a practical settlement between the capitals. Ottawa agreed to acknowledge Quebec's right to direct communication with the Agency secretariat, and yet this direct communication could occur only if the governments concurred, which amounted to saying that Ottawa was still able to scuttle it. There was recognition too of the possibility of Quebec's exercising a right of veto over the Canadian vote, a right that had been challenged in the course of negotiation. Naturally this veto could be employed only in votes on issues within provincial jurisdiction. Moreover, and contrary to what federal officials implied earlier, the Quebec-Ottawa agreement could not be used *mutatis mutandis* as a model for similar arrangements between Ottawa and other 'French-speaking' provinces. This agreement was specially confected for Quebec, apparently, since in some instances it took up much of the space reserved for Canada in the Agency institutions, a fact that excluded the possibility of other provinces' having equal representation with Quebec. These other provinces could still become 'participating governments,' but on different terms. The role was not reserved for Quebec alone, as federal orthodoxy holds it a bad thing for Quebec to be the only province admitted as 'French-speaking' in character. The fact that no other province has yet officially asked to be a 'participating government' — and for obvious reasons of common sense — does not alter the federal stand: one must avoid entrenchment of the principle that Quebec alone can enter an international Francophone organization as a participating government.

In such oblique ways did this settlement move the federal government towards an admission of Quebec's special character in Canada. We can be certain that the result fell far short of what could have been achieved with more vigorous use of the charter and a tougher stand generally. One key factor in the whole business, and one which would definitely have contributed to Quebec's genuineness as a participating government, was that of direct communication with the Agency. Here the potential impediment of 'mutual agreement,' achieved by conciliatory spirits in eleventh-hour telephonic intercession from the Quebec side, leaves Quebec still under the protectorate of an Ottawa that is no more enthusiastic than it ever was about the establishment of too cozy relations between the new Agency and the province which must be kept as much as possible 'like the others.'

Having expressed certain reservations, I must make an important assessment. Who won more in this affair, Quebec or Ottawa? Quebec's progress is relatively easy to measure. After the Gabon imbroglio and the sometimes epic confrontations that followed, it is possible, where it never was before, for Quebec to be at least an identified and distinct part of Canadian delegations to such international gatherings. At the same time it would be wrong to claim that Quebec has also acquired its own international presence, even in areas of its own constitutional jurisdiction. Let us merely say that events have made Quebec the federal government's senior counsellor for Francophone conferences.

Ottawa's advance has been subtler and harder to define, but basically more significant. Even if it has sometimes projected, because of the 'lack of respect' of one of its provinces, a reasonably bizarre and even comic international image in these manoeuvres, Ottawa has still managed to manipulate events so that it is much less handicapped than before in attending international meetings on subjects of provincial authority. The petty administrative complications raised, the shocks to protocol in having an identified provincial 'presence' in the Canadian delegation, have been more than offset by the now genuine possibility of Canada's more intense and significant involvement as a political entity in many aspects of international life. Through the process, Canada has acquired an official image that is more officially French-speaking than ever, thanks to Quebec and also to a certain adroit stage-setting that made federal as well as provincial delegates virtually all Francophone, at least in the beginning. Ottawa has been after this image from the moment Quebec first showed active interest in the awakening Francophone world community. Its acquisition, ultimately with Quebec acquiescence, is now used to prove that a distinct, autonomous Quebec presence at international conferences is no longer necessary or desirable.

8
A Piece of Leaven?:
Quebec in Federal Policy

Some people are prepared to see advantages in federalism when it allows the two levels of government to influence one another. They even view this mutual effect as the keystone of the system. In this sense federalism is held to work better in proportion as one government is stimulated to act by pressure from the other, or as the ideas and plans of the one give the other impetus or orientation. If, for whatever reason, Quebec succeeds in altering the course of federal policy, supporters of this view quickly decide a 'gain' has been made. Quebec has 'had its say,' and Ottawa has listened.

Recent history offers an illustration of this type of gain in the process of working out the Canada Assistance Plan. It would take too long at this point to examine that wide-ranging social program in detail. Let me limit myself therefore to the elements that are relevant to our present concerns. One of the Plan's major aims was to bring as much consistency and unity as possible to the variety of social programs then in force, begun at different times and focussing on specific beneficiary groups. It was hoped that by this means real needs would be better served, and the substantial sums allocated to the programs employed with greater economy.

Quebec's attention had been attracted by the same problem. It pioneered with a study of the entire issue in depth. The immediate cause of concern lay in the spectacular rise in expenditure for unemployment assistance between 1961 and 1963. A study committee on social assistance had begun its work in December 1961, and its report reached the Quebec government in May 1963. The burden of its message was that a more rational ordering was needed in Quebec's income-security measures, as well as a reorganization of its administrative arrangements. Except in a fairly indirect way the report received no immediate attention from government. Nevertheless it helped guide certain important moves of following years, such as the Social Aid Act and the reorganization of the social departments. The delays between presentation of the report and action on it can largely be explained in terms of changes of government in Quebec City, hence in ministers, over the decade of the sixties. Meanwhile the federal government showed great interest in the study's recommendations, even having the report translated into English. Ottawa moved more quickly than the Quebec authorities in bringing the spirit of the report to bear on the acts and programs for which it was responsible. It lay at the root of the Canada Assistance Plan idea. We were seeing the federal government carrying out reforms planned initially for the government of Quebec.

A comparable process occurred in the area of family allowances. Quebec put much time and energy into a review of the system, producing some concrete suggestions for substantial adjustment in levels of payment to benefit those families whose incomes and numbers of children called for more realistic government assistance. For the most part, Quebec's suggestions appeared in briefs to federal-provincial conferences of social welfare ministers, to be worked out in greater detail by the Castonguay-Nepveu Commission, whose report and related documents were issued by the Quebec department of Social Affairs in 1971. When they were first advanced in 1966, Ottawa bent all its efforts to prove the system then in use still offered distinct advantages. The situation later changed, however, and finally, with the publication of the Castonguay-Nepveu Report on Income Security, federal people began to lean heavily on Quebec ideas to bring Canadians a system transformed from top to bottom. We should add that Quebec itself was unable to move unilaterally on family allowances, as it did not administer the program, a circumstance that prompted Quebec in the years 1966-70 to demand its complete transfer from federal hands.

The Canadian public watching the conferences on constitutional reviews in February and June 1971 was thus treated to a rather curious debate. Quebec was claiming legislative and constitutional paramountcy in a domain, social policy, where studies initially prepared for the guidance of its own government had been picked up by Ottawa as part of the federal drive to regain the initiative. Confronting this position, Ottawa stated its determination to keep the upper hand in income security programs, adducing the large sums it allocated to them as proof of its indispensable role in redistributing the wealth of the country among the citizens, and as confirmation of its law-making prerogative. In addition, Ottawa skilfully stressed the reforms projected in its programs as implicit evidence of its innovative spirit and especially to highlight its deep desire to make policies in line with the objectives of the Quebec government. The proof: Ottawa's inspiration came largely from Quebec studies. Apprehensive of the future and impressed by so much federal good will, the other provinces found it more difficult than ever to see why they should support Quebec's constitutional stand on social policy.

Quebec's influence has been marked in another major federal policy field, regional development, where Ottawa's methods bear the strong imprint of the 'growth pole' concept advanced first, in 1965, by Quebec City. At that time the government had decided to divide the territory of Quebec into ten administrative regions with designated regional 'capitals' and 'sub-capitals,' where the idea was gradually to install such public services as social welfare branches, Quebec investment offices, hospitals, and so on. The underlying principle was that grouping these services in one or two locations that were relatively accessible to the whole population of a region would create an element of dynamism, foster a training function we would lack if government services were scattered through the length and breadth of the land. A first trial was made. In theory, Quebec policies for stimulating local investment and decentralizing industry were to derive support from a number of these 'poles' and on that basis get results in terms of regional diffusion: in practice, however, the policies were never fully carried through. As will be seen, the federal authorities jumped into regional development with both feet and with financial resources Quebec did not have. The 1966 change of government in Quebec itself brought challenges for the proposed division. It seemed that groups of electors in various counties were taking offence at their communities' not being chosen as regional centres. Conscious of this criticism, the new government maintained the scheme, but a few changes were made in regional capitals and sub-capitals.

Ottawa's regional policy was anchored to the concept of the 'designated region.' Using certain statistical yardsticks such as numbers of unemployed and job trends in a given period, Ottawa picked out specific areas in the country, generally groups of counties, as areas of insufficient economic growth. These were the designated regions. To industries locating there, or increasing their employment capacity, Ottawa awarded fiscal and financial advantages. The criteria for isolating these designated regions were applied uniformly across Canada. With time, however, experience plus criticism aroused by the implementation of a well-intentioned but half-baked policy brought notable improvements and a greater sophistication to Ottawa's regional thinking.

As its own thinking developed on the regional issue, Quebec challenged the concept of the 'designated region,' advancing instead the merits of 'growth poles.' Prime Minister Lesage introduced the topic in his brief for the July 1965 federal-provincial gathering. As Quebec policy was then in the process of being worked out in the Council of Economic Orientation, Lesage's comments more or less ignored the methods of selecting the 'designated regions' to focus rather on Quebec's responsibility in terms of regional development. 'The Quebec government controls virtually all the factors on which any regional policy must be based,' the brief read, 'resource development, municipal institutions, roads, and so on. Furthermore, administrative and sociological factors make it closer to its population than the government of Canada. This means that the Quebec government and the bodies it can create are much better able than the central government to carry out a truly effective regional policy.' Quebec considered itself as bearing the prime responsibility for regional growth on its territory. The idea was not new: Lesage had already expressed it in other public statements and he returned to it several times after the 1965 conference.

It was to confirm this responsibility and fulfil it in the most consistent possible way that Quebec officials had made a general plan of action which led, a few months later, early in 1966, to the division into regions with growth poles. Meanwhile Quebec's brief to the December 1965 federal-provincial conference on poverty attacked the policy of 'designated regions,' comparing it to the one Quebec itself was starting to implement. 'In the circumstances,' the brief asserted, 'definite opposition must inevitably arise between the federal scheme of designated zones and that now appearing in Quebec. We cannot help thinking that a program of subsidies, leading to the creation of low-paying industries in far-flung areas where there is little potential for later industrial development, is irreconcilable with our own objectives and harmful in economic terms.'

As might have been expected, the federal people defended their thesis and methods whenever they came under fire. Moreover, might being right, Ottawa's financial resources enabled it to carry out virtually any policy, passable or excellent. Quebec may have been correct in its judgement of the regional measures to be taken, but it lacked the means to translate them into reality. Progressively, however, as on other occasions, Ottawa found inspiration in Quebec studies. Eventually it reached a concept close to that of growth poles. This is no attempt to claim that all Ottawa's later regional policy springs uniquely from Quebec thinking and research, but simply to emphasize that the exchanges of views between Ottawa and Quebec have genuinely contributed to modifying the initial federal approach, resulting, through a gradual refining process, in measures better suited to local conditions and hence generally more effective.

In a totally different sphere Quebec has had a determining influence on the development of Ottawa's foreign policy. Somewhat brusquely perhaps, and clearly causing Ottawa some suffering, Quebec awakened Canada to the existence of the Francophone world community, still ill defined and in constant evolution as an international reality. Certain episodes in this arousal of federal consciousness are retold in other parts of the present book. The comments that follow are meant merely to sketch the broad outlines of Ottawa's conversion to that variety of biculturalism known as *la francophonie*. I shall speak later of bilingualism, that other aspect of the federal mutation.

It is an obvious fact that for almost a century, in foreign policy as in external trade relations, the Canadian central government has focussed almost exclusively on the Anglo-Saxon world. In all probability it would have kept on in the same way had Quebec not shaken the established framework. The signing of ententes with France and particularly their aftermath, Quebec's more or less official presence at international gatherings, its incursions into the area of external aid to the Francophone African nations, and, of course, its ministers' public policy statements, have prompted Ottawa to adjust the old balance to provide a much more considerable place in its foreign policy for relations with French-speaking countries. The passage of time might tend to give currency to the impression that this new inclination arose quite naturally at a given point. To accept this impression we would have to forget the real motive and immediate cause of it all: the behaviour of Quebec. We need look no farther: above all we must avoid blind belief in the federal rationalization of decisions Ottawa obviously made under Quebec pressure. Certainly there were French Canadians in Ottawa who had long wanted a reorientation in Ottawa's foreign policy to give greater emphasis to the French-speaking world. It might justly be asked how much longer these French Canadians would have made do with fond wishes, or private criticism of federal neglect, if Quebec had not intervened directly to upset the Anglo-Saxon balance that then seemed so firmly established.

At the present time, then, Ottawa is pursuing a foreign policy somewhat more respectful of Canada's bicultural reality. In the dialect of federal officialdom ('Europe,' in *Foreign Policy Serving Canadians*, 1970): 'Canada has undergone a long period of delicate compromise from which it has still not entirely emerged, and in the course of which our country has finally decided to express its essentially bilingual nature.' No Quebecker could take exception to this, for Quebec never claimed, in the federal context, a decision-making role in the French-speaking aspect of federal foreign policy. However, it spoils things a bit when Ottawa, stressing its recent conversion — still far from complete — labours to heap oblivion on the fact that Quebec actually forced it to revise its traditional practice, while on the other hand proclaiming the present orientation as if the unique copyright was Ottawa's own, in order to show Quebec, the other provinces, and the French-speaking nations of the world that the Quebec government would err in getting too involved in an area Ottawa considers to be an exclusive and eternal federal preserve. Among the many hypotheses one might posit over this issue the following is especially pertinent: how much longer would Canada's foreign policy feature the Francophone world if Quebec lost interest in it?

Another policy Quebeckers cannot condemn per se, but which obscures the true Quebec position, is that of bilingualism. For generations, certainly, French-Canadian nationalists have deplored the English unilingualism prevailing throughout the federal administration. With the same breath they have evoked the fate of French-speaking minorities in other provinces and even aided their survival financially. They heaped shame on provincial governments that restricted the rights of French-speaking citizens. In short, the spread and use of the French language across Canada has been, for practically a century, one of the major objectives of French-Canadian nationalism.

Then one day, at the beginning of the 1960s, this nationalism gave way to a new strain. From that time on the issue was less the extension of a French Canada, whose external elements dwindled with each successive census, than building the state of Quebec. Little by little, anxiety for pan-Canadian bilingualism gave way to anxiety for the status of the French tongue in Quebec. Some viewed this as a withdrawal of Quebec into itself. In fact it was a realistic reaction, begotten of a general and immensely profound awakening of self-consciousness.

In their 1968 election platform the federal Liberals called for a vigorous policy of bilingualism across Canada. Along with the fight against regional inequalities this figures as one of the main elements of the election propaganda surrounding the idea of the 'just society.' Believing — or at least giving the impression they believed — that they were resurrecting a century-old French-Canadian grievance, the Liberals took the policy to the country as a sort of separatism insurance. Their position was fairly simplistic: if we make Canada bilingual and fight against regional inequalities the threat of Quebec separatism will evaporate, for it battens on two facts: Quebeckers do not feel at home outside Quebec, and their rate of economic growth is inadequate. Diagnosis and prescription both totally missed the true problem. For several years Quebeckers had ceased arguing in terms of bilingualism in Ontario, or British Columbia: that was all over. Now it was Quebec they were thinking about. More or less unaware of the shift, the rest of Canada placed its trust in the allegedly beneficial effects for unity of a more aggressive bilingualism. At all events, though the country might be somewhat altered, they believed — and this was the important thing — that the federal system would keep functioning unchanged.

Returning to office, the Liberals could claim with reason that their bilingualism policy was directly descended from arguments many times reiterated in Quebec. There was this subtle difference, however, that they were former arguments not now abandoned but rather replaced in the scale of priorities by the determination to build a modern Quebec which would develop from a province into the veritable homeland of its citizens. Quebec premiers, notably Daniel Johnson and Jean-Jacques Bertrand, might frequently and distinctly state in their briefs to constitutional conferences — especially Johnson in February 1969 and Bertrand a year later — that they were certainly not against increased bilingualism across Canada, but that for them and all Quebec priority must be given to a new allocation of legislative powers. Stubbornly, Ottawa characterized itself as Quebec's spokesman in matters of bilingualism, and the result was profound misunderstanding on the part of the premiers of the other provinces, a misunderstanding that echoed right up to the time of the Victoria conference. Having used Quebec's alleged deep desire to live in a Canada that was bilingual from sea to sea in the campaign for its separatism-insurance policy, Ottawa then induced the other provinces to believe that Quebec was irrevocably attached to the embodiment of extended language rights in the Canadian constitution. Sure that they had thus solved once and for all, and fairly cheaply, the problem of a perennially dissatisfied Quebec, a number of provinces set aside their reservations — oddly, Newfoundland and Prince Edward Island were among them — and after mutilating the language provisions somewhat, agreed to have them inscribed in the Victoria Charter. They never understood why, after all that, Quebec turned the Charter down. Probably they still do not understand.

Let me sum up. The adherents of an optimistic federalism find wise parables in the influence Quebec has managed to exert on, for instance, the formulation of the Canada Assistance Plan, and conclude that Quebec has every reason to be content with a political system that allows member states an opportunity to guide federal decision-making in the desired direction. Not only, they say, does this pregnant conclusion apply to social measures such as the Assistance Plan, but with a little good will and imagination on Quebec's part a comparably decisive Quebec influence might extend to a number of other areas. Quebec could end up with a major role in the deciding of all federal policy and, considering its political weight and the pertinence of its points, virtually run them to suit its own interests.

In this light the development of the Assistance Plan and similar projects looks like a gain bespeaking vast new potential. If similar reasoning applied to areas such as defence of the country and regulation of exchange rates, there would indeed be justification, though perhaps not for hanging out the flags, at least for self-congratulation on the weight a province like Quebec can wield in the deciding of strictly federal policies. But when Ottawa policies affect areas of provincial jurisdiction in which the federal authorities choose to meddle, it is hard to understand the satisfaction experienced by those who cry that Ottawa accords a sympathetic reception to the proposals of the provinces. We should rather be astounded at the federal meddling.

In the case of family allowances, Ottawa was relying on de facto jurisdiction conferred by its spending power. Quebec, for its part, wanted, not influence at moments of more or less open crisis, but legislative paramountcy. Ottawa's anxiety to run the programs in accordance with Quebec's ideas was dictated by a desire to be able to claim that recognition of Quebec's constitutional paramountcy was unnecessary since in concrete terms its wishes were being complied with. Guarantees are still lacking with regard to the respective powers of Ottawa and Quebec in social affairs. The stand was similar in regional development. Quebec has not changed its view, but with the establishment of the federal department of Regional Economic Expansion and the magnitude of the sums available to this department, as well as the interventionary measures at its disposal, the Quebec government is relegated to a mere supporting role in this aspect of economic policy. Behind the smokescreen of regional development and the local programs issuing from it, Ottawa can as easily get involved in highways as in the restoration of historic monuments, or urban renewal. Regional development policies are proving among the subtlest and most effective methods of interference at all levels. The Quebec Planning and Development Board that hoped to control federal investment by wily contrivance and better knowledge of local economic problems has turned out to be nothing but an Ottawa arm in the bosom of the Quebec government. For, after all, Ottawa has the cash.

Completing the 'image' of regional policy, we must add the possibility of this federal aid being hedged in by conditions similar to those found in aid programs for underdeveloped countries. Not only has Ottawa policy in this area failed to buttress the power of the provinces, notably of Quebec, but there is also a very real risk that it may come to be used to propel a province in the direction Ottawa wants. And conditions attached may be of orders other than economic. On 28 February 1972, the papers reported that Secretary of State Gérard Pelletier had clearly insinuated that the federal minister of Regional Economic Expansion could show less generosity to New Brunswick if the municipal leaders of Moncton did not let themselves be persuaded to install an acceptably bilingual policy in their 35 per cent French-speaking community. The portfolio's incumbent gave his colleague the lie the next day, but the implication had been broadcast nevertheless. Moncton's unilingualism is certainly hard for French-speaking Quebeckers to excuse; but to what degree would federal pressure, summoned to correct the situation, be excusable? The day may not be far off when it is on Quebec that Ottawa wants to impose conditions that have nothing at all to do with the development of regions. Who can say that such is not already the case in private conversation between Ottawa and Quebec representatives? In this sense, the federal policy of regional economic expansion could gradually turn into a regional program of federal political expansion.

Quebec shows Ottawa the way? We have just seen how.

9
End of a Dream:
The Constitutional Review

Books could be written on the constitutional review: its origin, its verbiage, its development, its finale. Through the public statements it incited, the men involved in the discussions, and the abundant press attention it received we could reconstitute the pilgrimage of a land in search of itself, Canada, and another beginning to find itself, Quebec. For the moment I shall limit myself to an analysis of the significance of the 'gain' which some have attempted to see in the very fact that the constitutional review could be launched.

Daniel Johnson was the first of Quebec's leaders to call openly for a new Canadian constitution. 'The best way to get equality for the French-Canadian nation in a truly binational Canada,' he commented in January 1965, 'would be to lay the ground immediately for Quebec independence, which will be inevitable if a new constitution is not passed.' At that time his Union nationale was the official Opposition, looking around for a success formula. For this reason observers heard Johnson's suggestion as a kind of vaguely pre-election manoeuvre. Virtually no one took it seriously at the time. Events conspired to make Daniel Johnson prime minister of Quebec, however, and once in office he stood by his earlier statements. A relatively important political separatist movement had already appeared in the Rassemblement pour l'indépendance nationale, or RIN. Various nationalist associations in Quebec that could be classified as moderate, for instance the St-Jean Baptiste societies, had also begun expressing serious reservations at their annual congresses, conferences, and so on, about the Canadian federal framework, and this had been occurring right from the beginning of the sixties. Their declarations earned a few news stories, sometimes headlines, and caused some reaction outside Quebec. Next to the differently phrased but consistent assertions of Jean Lesage, these declarations did something, if not to enlighten those we still referred to as our 'Canadian compatriots,' at least to impress them with the relevance of the question, 'What does Quebec want?' More or less co-ordinated statements by Quebec ministers added to the general effervescence of ideas, themselves general in nature, a note of official caution. Undoubtedly bombs exploding here and there broadcast our unease to the rest of Canada in their own special way. At the same time it is worth noting that a certain number of Quebec editorial writers had felt it appropriate to emphasize the faults in the Canadian constitution. They may not have been as widely read inside Quebec as their authors hoped, but they were certainly noted by federal government people and by intellectuals in the other provinces. To what extent was De Gaulle's 'Vive le Québec libre!' from Montreal's City Hall balcony inspired by all this? Did it influence the events that followed? Probably no one will ever be able to say with any accuracy.

In any event the varied and persistent evidence of unease in Quebec at last prompted Premier John Robarts of Ontario to call a conference of provincial leaders in Toronto during November 1967. The meeting would give partici-pants — and by television, the public — a chance to think about its 'Confedera-tion of Tomorrow' theme. It was impossible, however, to turn it into a session of constitutional review. Prevailing thinking then ran much more in terms of peaceful co-existence of French and English Canadians, bilingualism and regional disparities. Even so, Ontario's move failed to win approval from the federal authorities. Whether Robarts had unrevealed reasons of his own for seeking the leadership in a challenge operation the inevitability of which could not, perhaps, have been realized at the time, no one now, apart from Mr Robarts himself, can tell with certainty. Anyway, from the Confederation of Tomorrow Conference we came to the constitutional review, and some have wanted to see that smooth interprovincial operation as having altered federal policy, even going so far as to assert that the provinces, as federated states or constituent parts of Canada, were in this case as in many others able to force Ottawa to move in the direction they desired. This is incorrect: beyond the fact that they did not meet in Toronto to remodel the constitution, later events showed that, except for Quebec, the provinces had little quarrel with the BNA Act. If at last, despite their initial hostility, the federal authorities agreed to engage in the review, it was partly to show the Canadian public how unsuitable it was for provinces to involve themselves in the general problems of the country in the absence of the 'national' government, and partly also to avoid their getting into the habit of creating disturbances whose fall-out might, even inadvertently, affect Ottawa's jurisdiction. Where a dispute of any kind arose it was up to the central power to take part, give guidance, and if possible turn the affair to its own advantage. In any case there had to be a federal reaction at some time or other to the stand maintained now for a number of years by Quebec. Ottawa could not remain indefinitely outside the great debate that was troubling an important province of Canada.

In February 1968, therefore, the first constitutional conference was called by Prime Minister Lester Pearson, who took the chair. Subsequent conferences witnessed a growing federal leadership until the time when, sensing support from virtually all the English-speaking provinces, Ottawa brought out the Victoria Charter. The charter was a tour de force. Certainly the constitution could be repatriated, revised, modernized, but the basic balance of the country, or to put it more accurately, the imbalance that prompted Quebec to challenge the existing allocation of power, would go unchanged. Unfortunately or fortunately, depending on one's point of view, the Victoria Charter was stillborn. Constitutional review miscarried spectacularly in June 1971. And the BNA Act went unamended, to the considerable embarrassment of a federal government that had typified itself before the voters of 1968 as the team to solve the Quebec problem by ushering in a 'just society,' and to the equally great discomfiture of a Quebec government to which the fortunes of the polls had bequeathed the problems of an emergent state when it would have been so much simpler, and more in its line, to assume the day-to-day administration of a peaceful province.

So it was that in the night of 22-3 June 1971, Quebeckers learned that their government had just said 'no' to the Victoria Charter. The news was comforting. Still, that 'no' was to kill the constitutional review Quebec itself had wanted. It was a curious finale for a process inaugurated amid so much hope and which had then lasted for over three years. Up to the last minute, even during the day of 22 June itself, federal representatives were staunch in their conviction that Quebec would accept the charter. Many in Quebec worried about their premier's true inclinations: it was wondered how far his quest for 'paying' federalism and his avowed wish to avoid 'pointless conflict' with Ottawa would take him towards endorsement of a federal proposal whose family resemblance to the notorious Fulton-Favreau formula was all too obvious.

Yet when the reply came, it was negative. To all Canada it spelled failure for an enterprise that had been much talked about and involved the more or less enthusiastic participation of all governments in the country. How did we manage to produce a fiasco of such monumental proportions? Might it not be because from the outset the two main interested parties, Ottawa and Quebec, were talking about different things? Might it not be because of incomprehension, misunderstanding, or, as we sometimes put it, lack of communication? In fact there were all those things, but there was a good deal more besides. Let us look at the facts a little more closely.

In calling for a constitutional review, Quebec wanted a far-reaching reform of the Canadian political structure. This aim stands out in all statements from the prime minister of the day, Daniel Johnson. It is simply not possible to fall into the misapprehension of thinking that Quebec was looking for mere adjustments.

To carry through a true reform in depth, the constitutional review would have to include challenge to the current allocation of powers between the orders of government. This is why, starting in 1968, all Quebec briefs stressed what was considered as a priority issue. Every time there was a chance between 1968 and 1971 the same priority was maintained and reiterated, by Bertrand as well as by Bourassa.

In challenging the division of powers, Quebec knowingly raised three much vaster issues at the same time: Quebec's place in Canada, Ottawa's role in Quebec, and the very nature of the Canadian political system. Quebec thought the premiers' constitutional conference could be the ideal and normal forum for considering such basic issues. It stirred up developments it hoped would yield rich results, and gave all Canada a unique opportunity to enter its second century in a new form, better adapted to contemporary social and political conditions. In this sense, Quebec's stand arose from a highly pro-Canadian orientation.

Nor did Quebec reach the negotiating table with its proposals in definite and final form. It was feeling its way, and its government did not want any irretrievable commitments at a time when Quebec's own political development was still far from clear. It began by enunciating certain governing principles, principles some hastened with justice to qualify as too vague. Quebec made more concrete suggestions later on. Virtually never did it have the chance to explain them in depth, have them criticized and reformulate them, since the division of powers never came under discussion except in a tangential way.

Quebec's approach found no favour at all with the federal people and it confused the other provinces, since they could see no major problem in the present constitution. Ottawa was never after an exhaustive reform of Canadian federalism. It saw no necessity for it, and the view was buttressed by federal fondness for the belief that Quebec's stridency emanated from a noisy but minority element of its population: the intelligentsia. Ottawa was very likely sincere in imagining that with the arrival of a government other than that of the Union nationale, or even simply of another premier from the same party, the constitutional question would fade into the background in Quebec itself. Ottawa could not have accepted the existence of a serious political problem in Quebec, or seen things as they were seen in that province, without at the same time casting doubt on the premises of its own agenda, the increase of bilingualism and the fight against regional disparity, through which it counted on satisfying the age-old grievances of French Canada.

Since we were moving towards constitutional reform anyway, it would be better, Ottawa thought, to guide it in such a way as to make it useful to the federal cause. Now it was axiomatic that the BNA Act needed modernizing, if only in language. Moreover it would have to be patriated at some time or other, so it could be amended in Canada. Why not see to it right away? Finally, why not make use of the circumstances to confirm Ottawa in powers it was exercising only indirectly at the time, but which it imagined it required in order to discharge its responsibilities as 'national' government? For all this a working plan was needed which, without formally ruling out discussion on the division of powers, would suggest other priorities more consistent with federal policy. It turned out to be equally necessary to elaborate a neo-federalist doctrine for the future; hence the publication of several working papers.

So it was that right through the forty months of constitutional review Quebec and Ottawa were arguing in parallel, Quebec continuing to hope for basic discussion of power sharing and political reorganization, and Ottawa trying to move as far as possible along its chosen path while at the same time being careful never to admit the constitutional problem in its full-blown political dimension. The other provinces, little concerned with constitutional problems, had no serious objection. Quebec, having gone through three premiers since the start of the review, and persuaded latterly that nothing would truly be resolved without agreement on the power issue, had resigned itself to the fact that the constitutional conference would first consider questions such as official languages, basic rights, the Supreme Court, regional disparity, taxing and spending powers, etc. The process began dragging, or seemed to: in English Canada especially, editorial writers gloated over the sparseness of solid results. Everywhere there was criticism of slowness and lack of consensus. In Quebec, independentist associations that had never put any faith in the success of the review process were singling out its pandemonium quality for ridicule. Following the September 1970 conference the federal government decided to bet everything on the leadership it had assumed in an attempt to step up the pace of events. From that moment we were locked on the course that wound up in the impasse of Victoria.

At that September gathering, the first Bourassa attended, it had been agreed that the work of review could be accelerated by bilateral negotiation. Quebec vaguely understood this to mean that there would be more discussion with Ottawa in the absence of the other provinces. At last there seemed a chance of getting at crucial issues frankly and directly. For Ottawa, however, as became clear later on, the expression 'bilateral negotiation' had a different meaning. A federal team under the justice minister would tour all the provinces armed with specific constitutional proposals in areas chosen by Ottawa after a few preliminary conversations with provincial representatives. The federal government would thus be the only one to know each province's reaction to the proposals and be to each the interpreter of the others' views, especially of Quebec's.

What this was intended to achieve was an initial and partial revision of the BNA Act for the following June's conference in Victoria. Here was a first federal blunder. Given its stand, Quebec could not go along with a truncated revision. But Ottawa was absolutely set on having something to show, and did not linger over subtleties. Provinces were offered a package deal which would, reading from the federal scenario, cement agreement on the following fronts: patriation of the BNA Act and the amending formula, basic and language rights, the preamble of the constitution, regional disparities, the mechanisms of federal-provincial relations, the Senate, the judiciary power, and international relations. One will already have noted the absence of any mention of the allocation of power, except as concerned international relations. In this latter case the federal government agreed to discussion, not because the subject normally arose under the rubric of division of powers, but because Ottawa was experiencing serious difficulties with Quebec, difficulties it wanted solved as soon as possible and to its own advantage; hence the priority of that issue.

It was December 1970 when federal authorities brought their list to Quebec City. Prior to touring the other provinces, they saw the wise course as beginning with this test, to enable them to tell the others that Quebec agreed with the package deal. Faithful to a venerable behaviour pattern in such circumstances, Ottawa detailed its plans to Quebec representatives known as more manageable than the usual negotiators, hoping by this means to better persuade the government of the cogency and appropriateness of the deal. Here was their second blunder. The contacts they chose, though more manageable, were pre-eminently ignorant of the entire constitutional issue, never having taken a conspicuous part in Quebec-Ottawa discussions on the subject. Nor did it occur to them to bear their tidings in confidence to more experienced men. Instead they took Ottawa's offer straight to Prime Minister Bourassa. As it happened, they had no idea that the federal list corresponded in every respect to the constitutional priorities established by Ottawa nearly three years before in the White Paper available to the public under the title *Federalism for the Future*. Acquaintance with this well-known piece of information would at least have given them some understanding that in calling for debate on the basis of such a package deal they were urging their government to fall in with federal priorities it had so far been rejecting. The story is not told here to throw blame on Bourassa for turning around and giving Ottawa the idea that he was not opposed to its plan — in any case as the leader of a new government he had a perfect right to do so — but we may regret that circumstances put him in that position without possession of the relevant portions of a dossier whose political importance was not particularly hard to work out.

Ottawa can hardly have believed its ears. For the first time since the beginning of constitutional review Quebec was being more 'reasonable' in its demands. The luggage of the justice minister's cross-Canada mission would now include a list of proposals to be sold to other provinces on the basis that they had suited Quebec. In Quebec City, meanwhile, things were not so clear. We were obliged to realize that without exactly falling into a trap we had at least marched a little too light-heartedly over ground that was, to put it mildly, poorly lit. Already at the September conference Quebec had imprudently, to avoid displeasure to other governments, agreed that the emphasis would be placed on the search for the amending formula, thus reversing its own former stand and leaving the way open for disputes like those surrounding the Fulton-Favreau formula back in 1964-5. We had to get back the lost territory before it was too late, and again raise the essential problem of division of powers. But how? Were we to return to the Johnson style and speak of 'equality or independence'? The new government's style, its image, its 'unequivocal federalism,' were ill suited to such a strategy.

The circumstances handed us the solution. For a long time the federal government had been broadcasting its intention of modifying the Canadian family allowance system. In Quebec the Castonguay-Nepveu Report on Income Security was near completion. It contained an entire series of proposals the implementation of which could radically transform, not only individual programs like family allowances, but the whole of social policy. Quebec was in an excellent position to carry discussion into that area. Beyond the quality of its research and the intrinsic value of the desired reforms, Quebec's stand displayed a flawless continuity from the Tremblay Report of 1954 through the subsequent Liberal and Union nationale régimes. Moreover Claude Castonguay of Social Affairs, who would be handed Quebec's case to argue, was a prestigious and respected minister of undoubted ability.

It was finally resolved in a Cabinet session at the end of January 1971 to demand that division of powers in social policy be placed on the agenda of the constitutional conference set for that February. A few days before this we had rushed into print with a portion of the Castonguay-Nepveu Report dealing with income security. In mid-January the minister had also given a key speech to the Ste Foy Richelieu Club on his ideas regarding social policy and Quebec's constitutional stand. They were reiterated the following week at a conference of federal and provincial social welfare ministers in Ottawa. The pressure was on: the imminent constitutional conference had just taken a new tack. Quebec had regained a measure of initiative and introduced a highly disquieting element into the federal game. By its very nature the issue Quebec formally proposed for debate, something Ottawa could not refuse, ran to a multiplicity of implications in the economic, social, administrative, judicial, and political spheres. It became a Trojan horse. Once it was inside the conference room, the debate on division of powers could not be sidestepped. I must also admit that the manoeuvre had elements of experiment. Was Ottawa really so adamant regarding a challenge to the present distribution of power? Some in Quebec suspected as much. We were certainly going to find out, first in Ottawa that February, and then that June in Victoria.

Quebec's exposition at the first of these meetings was heard by the other provinces with attention and misgiving. Ottawa, for its part, recognized the immense interest of the Quebec proposals and virtually congratulated Castonguay on his audacity and cogency, concluding that it did not seem at all impossible to bring the reforms proposed by the two sides into harmony. Their objectives were, Ottawa said, basically the same. In short, Ottawa placed immediate emphasis on the income security programs and a damper on the constitutional changes Quebec hinted at. Men of good will could surely come to an agreement on mutual wording for the programs, and was that not the important thing? Nevertheless, in the face of Quebec insistence, it was agreed to mention in the final communiqué that later bilateral meetings on these subjects would also bear on their 'possible constitutional implications.' Since these were admitted as at least 'possible,' Quebec seemed relatively satisfied. The federal government was committed to very little, however.

Numerous bilateral meetings did take place at the ministerial and official levels over the period from March to June. The Quebec and federal family allowance plans had to be harmonized: from now on the problem would be expressed in those terms. The federal minister lost no time in stating that he was without a mandate to review the constitution: his desire was to reach a mutual accommodation, but solely as regarded programs under consideration by the two sides. The constitution was for Victoria in June. As in the 1964 pension talks, Ottawa made substantial changes in its own plans, picking up several of Quebec's ideas. The drift was evident from the outset: remove Quebec's reason for complaint so that when the constitutional demands came up it could be told: 'But why insist on changes in the constitution? You can perfectly well see that we reached agreement without that. We changed to fit in with your objectives. What more do you want?' Ottawa would then be in a good position to claim Quebec was not being very reasonable, while the basic difficulty, the guarantees Quebec was after, were systematically shelved.

When the Victoria conference agenda was drawn up in June, Ottawa took significant pains to list 'social policy' among the non-constitutional subjects for discussion. The constitutional headings that did appear were, as if by chance, the same as those in the December package deal. Quebec's protests were half-hearted: some of its representatives, convinced Ottawa would yield no part of its prerogative in social policy, whether recognized, acquired, or merely implicit, decided it would be better not to make too much fuss, as this would spell failure for the conference. In other words, there was risk of damage to the December deal, something to be avoided at all costs, for, these men believed, the Parti québécois would then logically be able to claim the constitutional review was leading nowhere. This line of reasoning led to the curious notion that, because of the existence of the Parti québécois, the initial Ottawa plan absolutely had to go through, even if this amounted to a denial, for Quebec at least, of the whole point of constitutional review. There was no thought for the existence of a reality called Quebec, which rose above parties, québécois or not, and in whose name, years before, its government had demanded a re-examination of the structure of Canada. Such considerations were distant for a while in Victoria, and we were very close to a break in a political continuity that has nothing to do with the alleged wilfulness of a handful of technocrats, as Ottawa has claimed, but which has been taking root for generations in a soil that is authentically Quebec's.

In confidence, a few weeks before the Victoria affair, the federal authorities had sent each province a draft 'Constitutional Charter, 1971.' The document was not solely an Ottawa product, although federal influence had been strong: groups of officials in each province had gone over it, and the text incorporated suggestions from all over the country. In the weeks before Victoria, some preliminary changes had been made on the understanding that premiers would have their chance to pronounce on the most disputatious passages at the conference itself. The original headings were: preamble, political rights, language rights, the provinces and the territories, regional disparities, federal-provincial consultation, revision of the constitution, and modernization of the constitution. It will be noted that there was no mention of social policy, considered as 'non-constitutional.' The measures in question would call for simple technical accommodations requiring no change in the text of the BNA Act, or more specifically in section 94A, the very one that covered social policy.

With this in mind Quebec sent telegrams to the governments of the other provinces as well as Ottawa on 11 June, three days before the conference opened, to explain its constitutional stand on social policy. The explanation had in fact been requested at a federal-provincial gathering of 6-7 June by a number of provincial people interested in briefing themselves on the Quebec view. It had also been agreed that Ottawa would do the same. It so happened, however, that without Quebec's knowledge Ottawa communicated instead with all the so-called 'have-not' provinces, that is with all except Ontario, Alberta, and British Columbia, in some cases using a high federal official. Ottawa's message attacked Quebec's position and 'proved' how financially tragic its acceptance by those provinces would turn out to be. Each document was drafted specially for the province-addressee and delivered to either its premier or its social welfare minister. If required, the federal emissary could add an exegesis which may be imagined to have held little in the way of reassurance for the provincials.

This whole operation was supposed to be kept secret. Unhappily for the federal government, the Quebec delegation was informed of it during the Victoria meeting, and even had a peek at one of the messages that were supposed to be so devastating and convincing. The document explained the Quebec stand in its own way. Among other things were described: (1) how many millions of dollars the province would lose if Quebec's wishes were granted, the loss arising from the difference between its contribution to Ottawa and payments coming back to its residents under family allowance and guaranteed income supplement programs; (2) the danger that Quebec and the 'rich' provinces, those contributing more than their residents received back, might want to take advantage of Quebec's proposal and the fiscal or financial transfers it involved to set up these two programs on their own, in which case Ottawa would have little interest in maintaining them for the rest (only 18 per cent of the population) and thus be inclined to drop them, at a substantial loss to the province; (3) the obvious possibility that Ottawa would lose all motivation for increasing family allowances as it had planned and announced.

The manoeuvre was crude, for it had elements of blackmail, and moreover it spread a false idea of Quebec's position. For the specific purpose of avoiding loss to provinces Quebec had always proposed that a province legislating on family allowances, for example, should be able to do so only on the basis of the sums that would come to it if the federal program were still in force. This manoeuvre on Ottawa's part was clearly aimed at dividing the provinces against the less than probable eventuality of their being tempted to go along with Quebec. Besides, the method of divide and rule was not employed by Ottawa solely in the case of the provinces. For months it had been treating the Quebec proposals as Castonguay's own. Was this merely a slip of the tongue, or were they anxious to give currency to the idea that Bourassa was not especially enthusiastic about his minister's constitutional opinions?

Tension ran high at the Victoria meeting. Probably against all reason, the Quebec delegation kept hoping that recognition would at last be given, either with support from other provinces or a sudden illumination on Ottawa's part, to the constitutional paramountcy of provinces in social policy. For Ottawa the proposed charter was the culmination of over three years of discussion, and could, if accepted, show the whole country that the Liberal régime had made substantial progress in negotiations. Other provinces were fairly ill informed as to Quebec's main reservations, since their chief contact had been Ottawa. They were also persuaded that a Quebec Liberal government, known to be disinclined to confrontation and moreover distinctly federalist, would easily agree with another band of Liberals from Ottawa. They sincerely expected agreement on the charter to crown the review and mark the conclusion of its first intensive stage. For them, as for certain federal people, once the charter was adopted the review could be picked up again from time to time in years to come. The charter did deal with amendment, an issue unsolved up to this time, and since the constitution could henceforth be altered at will there would no longer be the need to devote to it, as they had done since 1968, such long, exhausting, and occasionally boring premiers' conferences. Other subjects could be discussed, subjects of more immediate interest and practical consequence.

The stakes were high for both Ottawa and Quebec. To move discussion along more rapidly, Ottawa suggested the premiers meet alone and without interruption behind closed doors. The closed meeting lasted about nine hours, from 11 am to 8 pm. In reality, though, the day was longer: premiers had met with ministers and advisors at 10 and would not break up afterwards until around midnight, 14 hours later. In addition, a group of officials stayed behind to put the finishing touches on the charter, and did not leave off until around 3 am. Eating as they worked, delegates did not leave the British Columbia legislature, the site of the conference, for the entire day. One had the feeling that the conference was not going to be allowed to end without agreement. Since that time, some have advanced the theory that the premiers' closed conference had as its sole purpose to bring decisive pressure to bear on the prime minister of Quebec. We will likely never know if this was the case, but certainly Ottawa was anxious to get a consensus that very day.

In fact its insistence, no doubt inadvertently, was to give Quebec a major reason for refusing to ratify. We know that in its initial form the charter contained no provision on social policy. In discussion, Ottawa suggested a new version of section 94A of the BNA Act. In the jurists' opinion the revised wording did not give provinces the paramountcy Quebec demanded. Ottawa could only reply that it could be proven one way or the other by test litigation. Obviously this was not good enough. Quebec was looking for something much more certain. Already warned of this possibility in February, the other provinces now began to believe Quebec was after a swap: a suitable 94A for the rest of the charter. Their own preference was for more detailed study of the section, and they did not at all like this seeming swap that might saddle them with constitutional powers and responsibilities they absolutely did not want. They also feared a secret deal between Quebec and Ottawa. The federal government made it clearly understood during the conference, however, that constitutional paramountcy, if it were bestowed, would not imply that Ottawa was automatically turning over to provinces wanting them the required fiscal and financial resources for the social measures that paramountcy gave them the right to plan and legislate. It was simply another way of refusing.

According to Prime Minister Trudeau, the charter, even with the revised section 94A to which Quebec objected, was to be accepted or rejected in its entirety; there was no question of keeping part now and leaving the rest to a later date. Ottawa was worried that if such a possibility were open, the entire process would have to be begun again, with some provinces opposing language rights, and so on. Most provinces could have delivered their verdicts on the spot, and in the affirmative. At the instigation of several premiers, however, and in the light of the document's importance, it was resolved to extend a 12-day period of grace during which time the project would be laid before each provincial Cabinet as well as the one in Ottawa.

Before that time expired, a number of provinces had signalled acceptance. Ottawa's own was obviously a matter of form. During the night of 22-3 June, however, seven days after the conference ended, the Quebec prime minister emerged from a meeting of his Cabinet to turn the charter down. The official reason was phrased thus in the government communiqué: 'This decision arises from the need to reach as complete an agreement as possible on clear and precise constitutional texts, thus avoiding transfer to the judiciary power of a responsibility that belongs pre-eminently to the political power, that is to those elected by the people. The texts dealing with income security thus leave an uncertainty that ill accords with the inherent aims of any plan of constitutional review. If that doubt were eliminated our decision might be different.'

In reality the Quebec government had finally understood that with or without the new section 94A, the charter was unacceptable. It produced no solution for the problems of Quebec, and its ratification would shelve the process of review. As far as other Canadians were concerned the charter was already in fact the new constitution, and would henceforth form part of a revised and modernized BNA Act. They asked no more than that. Finally — this factor received little notice at the time — Quebec's ratification of the charter would inevitably have meant formal acceptance of the present constitution, and thus of the division of powers laid down in that document. A mechanism for patriation had been devised. The Victoria Charter also contained an amending formula. All this meant that with Quebec's assent they would have brought back from London, complete with all the serious drawbacks it had for Quebec, a constitution which no Quebec government had ever dared endorse unreservedly. Despite all the reservations Quebec might have voiced to keep its options open, adherence to the charter would have been interpreted as adherence to the 1867 constitution. Later criticisms could have been met with remarks about how hard such an attitude was to comprehend, when in 1971 Quebec itself had helped patriate a constitution that was basically unchanged; unchanged that is, in respect of the allocation of legislative powers.

The Bourassa government had also discerned a groundswell of opposition developing in Quebec. Even in Victoria, the memory of the Fulton-Favreau formula haunted the Quebec delegation, and its evocative power had, it seems, stopped the prime minister short of irretrievable compromise in the presence of his colleagues from the other governments. This was astonishing to some, who saw in it a lack of firmness: they found it hard to understand how, with his majority in the National Assembly, and in their eyes an unconditional federalist, Bourassa could not issue an immediate, on-the-spot pronouncement in the charter's favour, even at the risk of having to go back to his Cabinet for ratification. They had seen him in Victoria, accepting, changing, even refusing passages of the charter, and concluded that his opposition was not total. At no moment in the course of discussion did Prime Minister Bourassa let it be openly understood that he might reject the whole document. When other premiers learned of the Quebec 'no' seven days later, they understood less than ever what was going on. They wondered whether there was not something else that explained Quebec's behaviour, and lapsed into conjecture. In fact, there was something else.

As we have already noted, the charter completely missed the real Canadian problem, that of the place of Quebec and the Quebec nation in Canada. What is more, Quebec's acceptance would have amounted to a denial of the problem's very existence. Instinctively, Quebeckers realized this. They were reassured by their government's refusal. For many, the prime minister was the hero of the day, defender of Quebec's rights at a tough conference that could not succeed. It could all have been predicted from the time, in December 1970, of the federal package deal, but it was not immediately perceived in Quebec City, where people persisted to the end in believing that progress might be made in Victoria after all. Quebec was caught increasingly in a dialectic that could only end in either submission or the failure of the conference.

In the long term, the impasse may turn out to have been a good thing. It is no longer possible for a Quebec government to resume discussion on the basis solely of the charter. By the end of 1971, in fact, there had been several federal approaches along these lines. Ottawa wanted to exchange the Constitutional Charter for a few concessions in the family allowances program: Quebec had left itself open to such attempts by citing lack of advance in social policy as its reason for refusal. If the constitutional negotiations are ever resumed, Quebec must be clear on the issues at stake and not afraid of making itself understood. In other words, if ever, in future talks, we must raise the problem of the sovereignty of Quebec, or special status, or simply a decentralized federalism, it will be essential for Quebec's listeners to be well aware of this, and not get the impression they are grappling with trick ideas and hazy notions the exact meaning of which Quebec itself cannot explain. Quebec must know what it wants to talk about right at the outset, and march into debate resolutely, not reluctantly, not to discharge a disagreeable duty as was the case after the April 1970 election, but to confront a deep and inescapable issue and above all to find a genuine solution.

Abortive though it may have been, the constitutional review still had to be gone through, and this was done because of Quebec. Some still try to find support here for the claim that Quebec can, if it wants to and if it expresses itself more persuasively, move the whole of Canada to share its concerns. We often hear that 'it's results that count.' We should perhaps distrust maxims, but not facts. The facts presented here can certainly not be used to prove Quebec's omnipotence in the Canadian confederation, or even its importance, though the cause be as serious as the future of a country.

I began this book with a question: what gains has Quebec achieved since 1960? The question was my starting point for as objective an analysis as possible of a number of events which, at the time they occurred, were able to induce the Québécois and other Canadians as well to believe that, since the 'Quiet Revolution' began, Quebec had made substantial advances on the federal-provincial front, strengthening its powers and securing new ones.

It is appropriate now to summarize the general tendencies of Quebec-Ottawa relations since 1960 as regards the consolidation or increase of the Quebec government's powers. From the analysis of the facts offered above, the following conclusions emerge.

None of the gains achieved by Quebec in the period was accompanied by guarantees of permanence. The federal government could contemplate the Quebec advances with equanimity only to the degree that they remained provisional from Ottawa's viewpoint, and to the degree also that effective federal opposition was impossible at a given moment. For these reasons, no such gain constituted a true precedent.

In virtually every case in which circumstances produced arrangements affecting Quebec only, the federal government was later seen trying by one means or another to reoccupy the terrain it had momentarily vacated. The drive for federal reconquest began to be noticeable especially in 1969, and was intensified in 1970 after the change of government in Quebec. Sometimes lack of firmness or consistency on the part of the Quebec government abetted these attempts.

For the most part, the Quebec gains were achieved only after major and open conflict with Ottawa, and practically never emerged from regular intergovernmental negotiation. These conflicts, which cannot be compared with straightforward normal tensions, were much more political in nature than they were administrative or financial; they brought into question the very role of the Quebec government, and often Quebec's place in Confederation as well.

Analysis of the gains themselves tends to temper any enthusiastic initial judgement. Certain apparent Quebec gains in fact gave more advantage to Ottawa, and over a longer term.

Quebec's financial and fiscal gains came only as a partial remedy for an existing imbalance that would have had to be dealt with sooner or later.

Most of the Quebec gains were made in provincial areas already under federal occupation or imminently to be so.

The Quebec gains are not so substantial as to have appreciably increased Quebec's political strength in relation to the central government or the other provinces.

The area of contention between Quebec and Ottawa is larger today than it was in 1960 and no basic problem has been definitively resolved during the period being examined.

The overall tendency revealed by the cases studied is thus the following. It has sometimes been possible to think that the Quebec government had succeeded since 1960, through negotiation with Ottawa, in enlarging its area of competence. In fact, most of the Quebec gains which were taken as meaningful at the time were achieved, not in areas that had previously been federal, but in provincial sectors that with time and the help of its spending power Ottawa had finally placed under occupation or was getting ready to take on. From this point of view the question has been less of a Quebec 'advance' into federal territory than of the temporary and partial suspension, from 1964 to 1968 approximately, of a movement of centralization in Ottawa of governmental control mechanisms. At the same time all Quebec gains achieved in this short period, and achieved generally in federal-provincial crisis, have been provisional in character: the exceptions are those that brought partial improvement to the division of fiscal and financial resources, and these applied equally to all provinces. These gains, then, came with no guarantee of permanence. Later, especially from 1970 on, Ottawa has been able to attempt the systematic reduction of these gains by trying to obtain confirmation for 'federal' powers that had been challenged. The overall result is that not only have the gains of the past decade or so brought Quebec no substantial increase in political strength, but also the problems cropping up between Ottawa and Quebec City are more numerous than ever. Moreover, the constitutional review Quebec insistently called for, and from which one could hope for solutions to various federal-provincial conflicts, ended in failure.

PART 2
ANSWERS

10
The Golden Calf: Ottawa's Suit

There is now widespread agreement that Quebeckers must have a government belonging wholly to themselves, one they control and whose action and policy can serve their particular needs and aspirations. The aim of this chapter is to show how the current working of the Canadian federal system greatly hinders the satisfaction of this necessity. My analysis is based on the Canadian experience of very recent years, which has thrown in higher relief than ever before certain techniques the Ottawa government can use, as occasions arise, to assert its predominance. The magnitude of the federal advance may vary with the time, of course, and Ottawa may use methods other than those I am about to describe. The differences are those of degree or of style, however, never of kind. Federal pressure on Quebec and the other provinces is a perennial phenomenon of Canadian life. The fact that it may have seemed more hesitant at certain periods, especially during the Quiet Revolution, does not mean it has gone. It is resumed with new vigour, we now realize, as soon as circumstances allow. This pattern will persist unless our system undergoes basic change.

Here then is not an exhaustive description of Quebec-Ottawa conflict, but an introductory glance at some recent events and a sketch of the political scenario which will then come under closer scrutiny. At first glance, Quebec-Ottawa skirmishing seems typified by contradictory, ephemeral gestures and statements by politicians from opposing camps who want to increase their own power and prestige. To display their sincerity and care for the common weal, these men have no hesitation in calling on a public that is completely unaware most of the time, not only of the bases of the points at issue, but also of the stratagems being employed by both sides. That element of the public patient enough to hold its interest in federal-provincial dispute from precipitous decline still sees at best only the most spectacular episodes. The impression left is hardly flattering for the governments concerned, and the pair of them are sometimes relegated to some deep crevasse of the collective subconscious. Exasperated by what they perceive as a now permanent misunderstanding, or persuaded Quebec's efforts are fruitless, some citizens decide they are better off giving their attention to problems that seem more immediate. Others, equally exasperated, opt for rejection of the system itself, consoling themselves with the thought that whatever Ottawa does, one fine day it will be put in its place. At this point they lose all active interest in the current alarums and excursions of Quebec-Ottawa rivalry. Sometimes the only people keeping up with events are a few politicians, a handful of civil servants, those journalists whose job is to do so but who harbour no illusions as to their readership popularity, and of course a minimal element of the general public. In such circumstances the struggle unfolds, one might say, with no real audience.

So far as Ottawa is concerned, this virtual absence of a public gallery has proven a useful seconder in its infiltration of Quebec prerogative. The federal authorities have endeavoured to avoid doing anything that might draw the Quebec public's attention to its control impulses. It has trodden very softly for fear of arousing some visceral defensive reaction, or fuelling a latent nationalism that would have made political capital for Quebec City. Absorbed over decades of experience and through numerous mistakes, this discretion was especially evident in the 1968-72 negotiations, during which Ottawa proved itself capable of some extremely skilful manoeuvring and polished techniques of approach and penetration. While the government of Quebec has not been in a position to counter the resulting centripetal movement, Ottawa has developed the ability to embark on vast programs overlapping Quebec's jurisdiction, and to do so with what has amounted to implicit support from a population that was prevented from realizing the full significance of the moves being made. Federal discretion has certainly not been synonymous with inactivity. Ten or twenty years ago, Ottawa was open to accusations of invading areas of Quebec authority, and had as a result to put up with vexatious reaction. With time, it has learned to pick its way around the pitfalls while sustaining the intrigue on a more extensive scale.

Confronted with the nationalist stirrings that accompanied the Quiet Revolution, Ottawa finally realized that a well-organized and ubiquitous publicity campaign might manage to convince Quebeckers of a number of useful truths. In this way, it was hoped, Ottawa would emerge in Quebeckers' minds as the capital of a country that was theirs from sea to sea, and cease to appear as the headquarters of a foreign and moreover an English-speaking administration. Like the Quebec government, the federal authority would shine as an 'every-day' government, there on the spot, caring for the citizen's welfare, worrying about his problems, and determined to solve them to the general advantage. Since 1969, Ottawa has put a good deal of energy into promoting in Quebec this image of a good, understanding, attentive father-figure. It has been one of the main objectives of Information Canada, an agency sharing in the general trend of image transformation that has made Air Canada of Trans-Canada Airlines, Statistics Canada of the Dominion Bureau of Statistics, and spawned a multitude of bodies ranging from Sports Canada to the Order of Canada.

Not to be too ephemeral, however, the new image had to be founded on something solider than greasepaint. Here is one of the arguments for bilingualism and the appointment of French-speaking ministers and high officials to posts previously inaccessible to them. Although they had disastrous consequences in a number of federal constituencies in the October 1972 election, 'French Power' charges levelled at Ottawa by certain Anglo-Canadian elements were used in Quebec to foster the idea that a species of 'quiet revolution' had taken place in the federal government, which emerged as an avenue of affirmation for the people of Quebec and a legitimate aspirant to a role formerly cast for the Quebec government alone. We saw a proliferation of clever devices, all grounded on the apparently inalienable right of the federal authorities to make direct payment to citizens anywhere in Canada. First it was Opportunities for Youth, then extended unemployment benefits to 'protect' more workers, then more generous family allowances for those in greater need, then the Local Initiatives Program, a revised and corrected 1972 edition of Opportunities for Youth, and, finally, New Horizons. To these must clearly be added the host of subsidies paid to private industry and those granted under regional development programs. The latter have been one of the most noticeable modes of federal presence in Quebec. In the guise of aiding regional growth, Ottawa began backing all manner of activities: parking lots, highways, the renovation of historic buildings, housing, institutions of learning, and so forth.

Under the hail of federal manna, and financially hard pressed, the Quebec government was driven to the point where, before engaging in any project, it automatically wondered what contribution it could expect from Ottawa. This was one of 'paying' federalism's least elegant aspects. Frequently, Quebec moves were planned as functions of anticipated federal funding, and projects rose in priority to the degree that they were financed from Ottawa. This does not mean that all programs thus implemented were by this token bad, or performed no useful service: that is not the issue. What it does mean is that Ottawa was increasingly in the position of exercising the real planning function, so much so that the Quebec Planning and Development Board became widely regarded as a branch of the federal department of Regional Economic Expansion right inside the government of Quebec. Nor should I forget in my list the liberal enterprises of the Canadian department of State which, besides Opportunities for Youth, organized student exchange, bursary, and various other grant programs.

All this largesse, and its manifestations were various, tended to prove how Ottawa pampered the citizens of Quebec. At least that is what Quebeckers had to be shown so that they would absorb the salutary lesson that Canadian federalism had very tangible benefits to offer them as well. Federal publicity was at work to entrench this idea, as, for example, federal advertisements broadcast on radio and television for a number of weeks in 1971 and 1972 on the enormous interest and benefit the LIP held for the average citizen. This advertising drive had its idiotic side, for instance when the federal people insisted that solid and permanent plaques be affixed to buildings, schools, or housing projects for the edification of present and future generations, blazoning Ottawa's financial contribution. Since Quebec City, although a contributor itself, had virtually never put up such notices, there were intergovernmental skirmishes that might have been amusing in somewhat different circumstances.

The 'battle of the notices' even reached the highway system. Ottawa insisted that when these new works were officially opened, federal ministers and MPs from the region, most particularly from the constituency, be invited and given a chance to speak. The federal people even went so far as to demand that the names of schools to which the federal government had contributed be selected jointly by Ottawa and Quebec City: they had to make sure the names used were those of deserving and orthodox Canadians. When Quebec-Ottawa conventions on participation in school construction came up for renewal, Ottawa insisted that Quebec commit itself, in the very texts of the agreements, to publicly recognize by plaques, notices, and other visual means the generous financial co-operation of the central government. The issue had attracted so much conflict that Ottawa wanted an acceptable 'normalization.' It was clearly indicated to Quebec that refusal would bring on a drought in federal grant money. Breaking out in numerous disputes towards the close of the Union nationale reign, the federal publicity conflict subsided with the arrival of a Quebec Liberal régime, and the sometimes obsessive pursuit of 'paying' federalism. There was more readiness to meet Ottawa requirements, providing the subsidies continued. Quebec City yielded and signed the proffered agreements, though a persistent element of passive resistance occasionally stopped federal advertising from fulfilling all Ottawa's hopes and expectations.

Confronting a Quebec government that was sensitive about its constitutional prerogative — more often the case with the Union nationale — Ottawa made sure to avoid the impression of a frontal assault on provincial sectors. 'Training' was the word used rather than 'education,' 'problems of urban growth' replaced 'municipal affairs,' the 'fight against unemployment' replaced 'social development,' 'community development' was the new expression for 'culture.' Ottawa could speak freely on any subject providing the terms it used did not ring suspiciously of those areas which Quebec, atavistically or otherwise, had come to regard as being within its own jurisdiction. The style changed when Ottawa was dealing with a Quebec government, the Liberal régime after 1970, that was more pliant before the imperatives of federal life in Canada. The very manner and stated motive of Ottawa's action supplied Quebec City with any excuses it might need in case citizens or pressure groups of nationalist tendencies took umbrage at gradual federal distraint of areas assigned to provinces by the BNA Act. Such a government had only to reiterate the federal fallacies, tacking on to them its own plea about the limited room allowed for manoeuvre, despite all its good will, by the current political and world economic situations. Within the administration itself, doubting ministers and officials were told that 'Ottawa would lose nothing by waiting,' but that for an initial period it was 'more profitable not to raise pointless problems,' and to make the most of the excellent personal relations between Liberals in Quebec City and Liberals in Ottawa.

In any event it was important for the Quebec government, whatever its political stripe, to be forestalled from effective opposition to federally originated programs even if they did affect areas that were normally provincial. The Ottawa strategy tended to be expressed in two main ways. Swift action would place the Quebec people on the defensive: they were then left with the ungrateful role of blocking federal policies that were objectively valuable and at the same time carefully 'sold' to the population in general. In the first instance Ottawa was, and still is, supported admirably by its general spending power, its more considerable financial and human resources, and certain constitutional ambiguities that are deliberately perpetuated. I shall return to this particular point. In the second instance Ottawa could merely announce that it proposed to attack, with the people's co-operation, such problems as unemployment, social alienation, pollution, or regional disparities. Who could fight the fight against unemployment? What Quebec government in the circumstances could voice objection to so well-intentioned a federal move? Ottawa would immediately have seized the opportunity, calling the people as its witnesses, to accuse the government of being backward, unaware of the needs of the day. Ottawa could insinuate that such a government, stalled as it was in outdated juridical considerations, intended to deprive citizens of money the central government was liberally placing at their disposal, and to which they had as much right as anyone else in Canada.

Having thus managed to pour funds into daycare centres, special courses for handicapped workers, leisure organizations, sports groups, theatre companies, and research programs, and thereby forging new and mercenary links between the citizenry and the federal authority; having spanned the gap between Ottawa and the individual Quebecker in ways whose own dynamic would in time enlarge their scope even more, Ottawa was then in a position to prove to any doubter its genuine concern for the daily problems besetting the men, women, and children of Quebec. At the same time it could refer to actions of a month, a year, ten years, or even a generation before, to claim de facto prerogative in areas not originally its own, and take every opportunity to consolidate and push on even farther. Allied with the federal way of thinking, this process has convinced Ottawa that its jurisdiction is firmly established in the areas of culture, social development, adult retraining, research, regional development, social welfare, urban affairs, and so forth. It is also possible for Ottawa to discover an 'interest' in education, since after all it pays for courses, gives grants for school construction, and sends teachers abroad. In short, all imaginable areas of human activity, especially those that will gain in importance as time goes by, feature now among Ottawa's active concerns. It may feel the need to intervene at any time: doing so with increased and further refined expertise, it will reply to anyone taking exception that the deed is already done, and it cannot be blamed for discharging its responsibilities as 'national' government with the greatest possible efficiency.

The 'precedent' technique was displayed in an interesting way when, in February and June 1971, Quebec demanded recognition of its constitutional paramountcy in social affairs. Ottawa did not open discussion on the issue of paramountcy as such, any more than it tackled the basis of the problem Quebec was raising. Instead, the federal people chose to make it quite clear that they were already functioning in the area Quebec lusted after, and had been doing so for a long time; that over that period they had poured enormous amounts into it, resolved a number of problems, and improved their policies from year to year; and that their equalizing presence was desired by the people of Canada. From this viewpoint it would take very little to make Quebec's stand look reactionary, inspired by the rejection of modern income security philosophy. Happily, we did not quite come to that point.

The federal use of 'precedent' can, however, lead in strange directions. It figures also in the perennial dispute over communications: in fact, whatever sector we consider, the federal government can claim authority by virtue either of what it has already done or of its role as 'national' government. It will agree, however, to leave provinces with those administrative sectors it sees as related to more or less routine supervision and management where policies have been installed and proven for a long time. The sheer flagrancy of a federal invasion in education has so far stayed Ottawa's hand, but the time will come. For the moment we will merely cite the *Canada Yearbook* for 1970-1: 'Some 60 departments and agencies of the federal government are participating in one way or another in the financing of instruction. ... The organization and administration of public instruction do not fall within federal jurisdiction. However, the federal government is intensely interested in the general level of instruction and qualification in the population, as well as in scientific research in Canada; it is conscious of the profound effects these factors have on the national economy.' Indirect influence has already proven very strong: Quebec's schedule for school reform was much swayed by the federal program of participation in capital expenditure for technical and professional training.

Ottawa would never have been able to engineer its entry into provincial preserves with such ease if it did not have three tactical weapons of great effectiveness: human and financial resources exceeding the provinces', the general spending power, and the existence of the grey areas of the constitution. When Quebec puts together a working group for any given subject it may designate for the job some three to ten ministers, officials, and outside experts. They devote part of their time to the study, but in almost every case they retain their usual administrative responsibilities. For the same work Ottawa will mobilize three or four times the number of people, several of them fully seconded from their departments. If after all this more experts are wanted they will be recruited without worry over cost. When Ottawa wants to launch a program, experiment, or innovate here and there, it is always easy to find the required million or so. In Quebec City a few tens of thousands are finally scraped up, and it is often realized at the outset that they will not be adequate to bring the projects to a successful conclusion. Destitute as it is, Quebec is even less able to contemplate such programs as Local Initiatives, Opportunities for Youth, or New Horizons.

The imbalance of power between Ottawa and Quebec is such that all competition eventually bears witness, barring accident, to the federal government's greater strength. Ottawa desires this imbalance not through wickedness or political pettifoggery, but simply because in its view the 'national' government must naturally be much stronger from all points of view than the provinces. It will then be in a position to secure such 'national' objectives as it decides may flow from its prerogative. Largely for this reason, Ottawa has been refusing any substantial transfer of resources to the provinces since 1966. Ottawa needs room for manoeuvre, and it is unhealthy in the federal view for any province, especially Quebec, to have too much freedom.

The instruments are there. The general spending power can operate to centralize power in virtually any sector, as we have seen, while the notorious grey areas of the constitution offer Ottawa a choice of avenues for leisurely infiltration of any and all areas not expressly assigned to the provinces of 1867. If conflict arises Quebec is awarded the burden of proof: it must show its right to act, and having done that, go on to demonstrate financial capability. Yet the government of Canada is as attentive to its legitimacy as any other government in the world, and likes to take the opportunity to base its moves on some sort of popular consensus. This is perfectly natural, and would call for no special comment if the process did not involve some more dubious practices. Especially in ministerial announcements and solemn policy statements, Ottawa officialese is full of open-sesame expressions whose merest reverberation, or so it seems, can suffice to clothe federal aims in the most devastating of finery. The objective is the same: to place the provincial opponent on the defensive while arming oneself with reasons so overwhelming, and so universally admissible, that they cannot be gainsaid. Hence the allegation that 'Canadians want' this or that, that the federal government wants to suit its policies to the wishes of 'Canadians,' or that 'Canadians' have a given right that it is Ottawa's duty to protect. No one has ever been able to say with certainty who these convenient 'Canadians' were, but no matter. When they are not up to the occasion or when the vocabulary needs varying, appeal is made to 'federal responsibilities,' another concept without precise definition, its meaning reflecting the federal necessities of the day. Where do the 'responsibilities of a national government' begin and end? There is little point in looking for borderlines. We are in a transcendental sphere, far out of reach of local administrations. One may recall the abundant use made ten or twenty years ago of flexible ideas such as 'national interest,' 'national unity.' To these worn-out ideas, their returns now sagging, have been added the 'Canadians' and 'federal responsibilities.' Ottawa always has a few expressions of this kind to justify or require intervention in areas supposed by poor ignorant souls to lie within provincial jurisdiction.

The slow but eventually devastating progress of the federal government has not been without incident, however. In several provinces, Quebec particularly, there has always been a political party or citizens' association to put forward another view. In Quebec, premiers Duplessis, Lesage, Johnson, and Bertrand, each in his own way, managed for a time to stem a number of federal rushes; they did not stop the wheel from turning but they did slow it down, either by advancing their own policies or by invoking Quebec's powers under the constitution. These acts of sabotage of the great federal design obviously angered and alienated Ottawa, which then felt it had to pick out the guilty parties. Ottawa knew the danger of frontal attack on Quebec. The reaction, borne out in the crises over conscription, was what was known in contemporary terminology as a 'common front' against the central authority. Thus did Ottawa decree the new truth: Quebec opposition to its aims emanated either from a handful of intellectuals who left the general public cold or from vindictive editorial writers, prejudiced and sensation-seeking journalists, union leaders looking around for a

'cause,' or separatist civil servants manipulating naive ministers. In short, the guilty parties were at most an infinitesimal proportion against a silent majority that was in essential agreement with the 'national' government, since nothing counted for that majority, Ottawa told us, but bread and butter. A further refinement of federal procedure, and this technique was picked up in Quebec City with the advent of the Liberals in 1970, was to ordain that 'constitutional questions interest no one' except, obviously a few impractical aesthetes. These issues have been subtly tied in with austere juridical concerns. If this were the reality it would have been right to do so, but the fact was and remains that the constitution is basically a political problem whose effects are much more regular a part of our lives than we tend to think.

As will be seen more at length in another chapter, the probability of effective joint action by the provinces is minimal. Ottawa devotes little effort to forestalling it. It needs only let the provinces do the job themselves. The divergence of their interests is generally enough to nip in the bud any common stand that might wring momentary embarrassment from Ottawa. It does not follow from this, however, that the existence of ten provinces in Canada is a neutral factor in the federal checkerboard. Their ideal function is as regional administrations, carrying out such measures as the central authority may devise, adapting them to local conditions. Yet they are useful in another and more political sense: Ottawa can arrange for views opposing Quebec's to be expressed through one of the other provinces, especially when it may be inadvisable for the federal government to advance them itself, or when constant reiteration by the same people may erode their credibility. Ottawa certainly does not have to make a special appeal to any one province to ensure contradiction for the views of Quebec. Most of the time, the federal purpose is served by quite simply making use of bilateral meetings to encourage whatever natural reservations a province may already harbour on Quebec's objectives. When the time comes for discussion of these objectives, usually in a federal-provincial conference, that province — there may in fact be several — will merely line up on the federal side and expound its position in such a way that all those present understand that it tends to undermine Quebec's. Ottawa may remain silent all this time. If Quebec insistence is too strident, the federal people may even use the reproving attitude of the spokesman province to imply to Quebec that its first job is to convince other provincial governments of the soundness of its ideas. This was the tactic employed at Victoria in the June 1971 conference, to thwart Quebec's drive for paramountcy in social policy. It has been seen at several other points over the past few years, particularly in the attempted rebuttal of Quebec's claims in international relations.

It is not hard to see how, in negotiating with Ottawa or the other provinces, Quebec often finds itself, putting it mildly, in an awkward position. Quebec faces an existing balance, acquired methods, customs, tacit norms and practices, in short an entire intergovernmental way of life that works against it in so far as it wants to change the rules of the game, the division of powers, or its own juridical status. If Quebec wants to behave otherwise than as a docile province, however slightly, it is very quickly isolated: no one will follow it or give it support for very long. Success in the face of all this, even incomplete or later challenged by Ottawa, can only be the result of accident or a devious energy no other province can muster. If Quebec's representatives display the slightest weakness the negotiation is almost inevitably headed for failure. Yet we may ask: what happens if Quebec is absolutely right, and comes to the table fully prepared?

In Quebec-Ottawa relations, the possession of objective rightness is not enough to secure acceptance of one's views. Checking off the evidence does not mean the world will see it. I may illustrate what I am advancing with the so-called 'good case,' in current parlance a watertight argument in which all a problem's aspects have been evaluated and arranged for the edification of the skeptic, all potential solutions weighed and the best chosen. In the frame of reference of this discussion, it means a case to be made before the federal authorities by a minister and officials all of whom are competent and perfectly well informed on all sides of the question as well as all possible objections to the stand. This amounts to saying that to earn its description, a good case must not only be impeccable but also escorted by a champion who is extremely solid and sure of himself. We do not have a good case merely because we are or believe we are right. It is a truth many Quebec ministers have learned at their cost. They thought vainly to impress Ottawa with energetic assertions, founded on brilliant intuition and clothed in generalizations as candid as they were sincere.

Over the past decade or so, Quebec has often had such good cases to present: the pension plan and contracting out of shared cost programs in 1964, France-Quebec relations from 1965 to 1967, the agreement on housing and urban renewal in 1967, Quebec participation in the Agence de co-opération in 1970 and 1971, constitutional paramountcy in social affairs during 1971 and 1972, and others of lesser notoriety. In some instances, as we know, Quebec succeeded in extracting gains, though Ottawa always later tried to recover any territory momentarily lost in circumstances favourable to Quebec City. Yet how is it that these 'good cases' have not brought undoubted and permanent success in every instance? How is it that in some, Quebec has finished with a resounding failure on its hands? The answer lies in the fact that apart from their intrinsic technical value, the solidest of Quebec's cases were all inspired by a concept of the Quebec government's role and an idea of Quebec's place in Canada that stood in absolute conflict with federal views. Seen in these terms, yielding to

Quebec's argument simply because of its quality and substance would mean acceptance of political stands that would shake the foundations of federalism as Ottawa understands it. This means in effect that Quebec's good cases come to grief, not because they have some technical fault that has escaped their authors, but because their success would bring elements into the Canadian political system to threaten the supremacy Ottawa is bent on conserving for the central power.

Drawing on the Canadian experience of 1968-72, I have outlined the general conditions in which the Quebec fight was being waged. Never before had Quebec's political power been so systematically savaged. On the Ottawa side, as circumstances allowed, there was the intention of taking the full responsibility of a 'national' government. Free rein was given to all the naturally centralizing tendencies of a federal administration. On the Quebec side, we witnessed the arrival in office of a party which either did not know how to face up to this centripetal force or else did not want to. Instead, they had worked out the philosophy of 'paying' federalism, which struck many as a rationalization in political terms of a mere lack of vision and firmness, but did offer Ottawa the advantage of a free hand. Together these two governments, the one in Ottawa and the newly provincial administration in Quebec City, undertook to convince Quebeckers of two new 'truths.' First, federalism as Ottawa conceived it could mean numerous material benefits. I have already referred to the careful publicity by which the central government, with passive collaboration from the province, put this notion in people's heads. In the end, many actually believed it. According to the second 'truth,' though it meant almost certain erosion for the Quebec government as a collective instrument, it was possible for Quebeckers to take up the reins of power in Ottawa and wield a decisive influence on the development of the entire country. In short, there was to be established in Ottawa a 'Quebec power' that could normally sit only in Quebec City. The October 1972 federal election showed how deceptive this notion was by the reaction, just as normal, from English Canada.

Repeated insistence from Ottawa and its spokesmen on the tangible advantages Quebeckers could expect from the central government is, in this view, a clear corollary of the spread of the independentist option in Quebec. It now seems obvious that Ottawa wanted to forge direct and mercenary links with the Quebec citizenry. Quebec independence would thus, it was hoped, become more and more difficult to bring about, since, among other consequences typified as disastrous, it would have the result of drying up ever increasing sources of lucre. This federal objective, concurred in by certain spokesmen for the provincial administration, has never been publicly recognized by Ottawa. And I have to admit that from the federal viewpoint there were other reasons for greater centralization and a more conspicuous role for the federal administration throughout Canada. After the minority governments of the past decade and Quebec's aggressiveness of the Quiet Revolution years, it was important for Ottawa to reaffirm its authority and confirm its predominance in the country's business. All these factors produced the intensive movement of federal penetration whose characteristics I have been examining. There is certainly nothing fortuitous about the events of 1968-72. They suit the logic of the present system.

11
The Gospel
According to Saint Ottawa

In any exchange of views parties will have a frame of reference, perhaps better termed an ideology, on which they directly or indirectly rely. For all that they may be illogical, their positions are always based on a certain idea of their roles and responsibilities. The political stands taken by Quebec and Ottawa are not products of chance, corresponding as they do to real needs and aspirations. We must determine whether they are reconcilable, if there is truly a possibility of agreement on basic principles.

It would be a great mistake to think that the failure of constitutional review in Victoria in June 1971 was purely the consequence of tactical errors committed by one side or the other in the course of negotiation. I cannot be satisfied objectively by this interpretation, which is especially convenient for the champions of unconditional federalism since it is silent as to the basic cause of the fiasco. By the same token I could not seriously pretend Quebec has made few gains over the past decade because its cases were inadequately considered. The explanation lies elsewhere, in the official Ottawa doctrine that began to emerge towards the close of the Pearson régime. The doctrine took shape over a period of time and was finally ready for publication in the first of the federal White Papers circulated at the time of constitutional review. It appeared in February 1968, under the title *Federalism for the Future*. The subtitle drew little attention at the time, but it is reasonably evocative: 'Declaration of principle and statement of the policy of the Government of Canada.' This is not, then, what we could call a 'working paper.' Moreover, from the standpoint of the federal government's strategy in constitutional review it is by far the most important of all the White Papers. Here is a detailed account of federal priorities, later enacted to the letter, as well as some extremely valuable statements of political positions and principles of government that shed dazzling light on the true Ottawa objectives. We in Quebec were wrong in 1968 not to take in all this paper has to offer. Probably its vague title, its theoretical content and unctuous style, its delicacy of expression and the apparent truisms strewn through it served as an effective screen for the important substance it contains. Certainly it bothered no one at the time. Yet everything was there: subsequent White Papers merely applied to concrete cases the basic opinions and postulates in this first official stand.

Federalism for the Future did not emerge that February by spontaneous generation. In his opening speech to the finance ministers' conference in September 1966 the federal representative drew on a similar body of ideas; later federal spokesmen were to intone these ideas like canticles. And earlier, even in his most conciliatory period, Mr Pearson had used the same broad themes to buttress his government against Quebec. In reality — and this is what we have to remember — the White Paper of February 1968 had nothing new to show in terms of political philosophy and thinking on the division of powers, for it was faithful in every detail to traditional federalist theory. Its merit is, in serving them up in a modern manner, to have made these theories even more consistent, and united them in a sort of Declaration of Canadian federalism that is accessible and handy to consult.

Here then, from pages 34-44 of *Federalism for the Future*, is the statement of principle that would direct the later examination of the division of legislative powers between Ottawa and the provinces. The italics are my own.

Discussions on the division of powers should take place, in the opinion of the Government of Canada, after the constitutional conferences have considered the other principal elements of the Constitution — the rights of individual Canadians, including linguistic rights, and the central institutions of federalism. We say this because *provincial interests and the interests of Canada's two linguistic groups are not and cannot be represented simply through the device of transferring powers from the federal government to provincial governments.* These interests are and must be reflected as well in constitutional guarantees and in the central institutions of federalism. It follows that a balanced judgement as to the powers required by the provincial governments for the primary purpose of protecting linguistic or provincial interests can only be made in the perspective of the constitutional guarantees and the representation of such interests in the central organs of government. To jeopardize the capacity of the federal government to act for Canada, in the name of protecting linguistic and provincial rights, when what is essential could be accomplished through constitutional guarantees and the institutions of federalism, would be to serve Canadians badly. *Furthermore, the division of powers between orders of government should be guided by principles of functionalism, and not by ethnic considerations.* Such principles can best be applied after issues concerning the protection of linguistic rights have been settled.

The Government of Canada would propose, therefore, that discussions on the division of powers take place at subsequent conferences. However, in anticipation of these discussions, and as a guide to the direction of the Government's thinking we believe we should place before the Conference some of the principles by which we feel we would have to be guided.

First, we are committed to the view that *Canada requires both a strong federal government and strong provincial governments.* The field of government now is so wide, and the problems of government are so many, that it is not a contradiction to speak in these terms. Governments themselves confirm this view when they argue that their spending responsibilities exceed their ability to raise revenues. There is another reason for achieving a balance between the powers of the federal and provincial governments: the freedom of the individual is more likely to be safeguarded if neither order of government is able to acquire a preponderant power over the citizen.

Secondly, the Government of Canada believes that there are certain areas of responsibility which must remain with the federal government if our country is to prosper in the modern world. *The Parliament of Canada must have responsibility for the major and inextricably inter-related instruments of economic policy if it is to stimulate employment and control inflation. It must have control over monetary and credit policy, the balance-wheel role in fiscal policy, tariff policy, and balance of payments policy. It must be responsible for interprovincial and international trade. It must be able to undertake measures for stimulating the growth of the economy, some of which inevitably and some of which intentionally will affect regional economic growth.* Without such powers Canada's federal government would be unable to contribute to many of the central objectives of federalism, including the reduction of regional disparity.

We believe that *the Government of Canada must have the power to redistribute income, between persons and between provinces,* if it is to equalize opportunity across the country. *This would involve, as it does now, the rights to make payments to individuals, for the purpose of supporting their income levels — old age security pensions, unemployment insurance, family allowances —* and the right to make payments to provinces, for the purpose of equalizing the level of provincial government services. It must involve, too, the powers of taxation which would enable the federal government to tax those best able to contribute to these equalization measures. Only in this way can the national government contribute to the equalization of opportunity in Canada, and thus supplement and support provincial measures to this end.

The Government of Canada believes it must be able to speak for Canada, internationally, and that it must be able to act for Canada in strengthening the bonds of nationhood. We have said what we think this implies in international matters. Internally it seems to us *to imply an active federal role in the cultural and technological developments which so characterize the 20th century. We acknowledge, of course, that the nourishment of Canada's cultural diversity requires imaginative provincial programs, as well as federal ones. But there is a role for the Government of Canada, too; indeed cultural and technological developments across the country are as essential to nationhood today as tariffs and railways were one hundred years ago.*

There are central areas of responsibility essential to the apparatus of the modern sovereign state — economic policy, the equalization of opportunity, technological and cultural development, and international affairs. There are among these, of course, areas of responsibility which are shared with the provinces — including cultural matters, regional economic policy, and social security measures. However to catalogue these now, or federal powers generally, would be to depart from a statement of guiding principles and to anticipate the discussions of future conferences.

The third principle which would guide the Government of Canada in discussions concerning the division of powers is that *most services involving the most immediate contact between the citizen and the government, and those which contribute most directly to the traditions and heritages which are uniquely provincial, should generally be provided by Canada's provincial governments. Strong provincial governments, able to adapt public services to the particular needs of their people, are as essential to meet the facts of diversity in Canada as a strong federal government is to the preservation of Canadian unity.*

The governments of the provinces have responsibility for education, and their own power to support technological and cultural development — so often associated with educational institutions. These powers play an important part in the flourishing of Canada's linguistic groups, and of the diverse traditions to be found in our country. We acknowledge, of course, that many of the institutions involved serve the nation as well as the province but this fact should not be allowed to diminish the capacity of the provinces to perform their role.

The Government of Canada believes that *the provinces must have the power to provide health and welfare services.* For instance, the provincial governments rather than the federal government should operate hospitals or public health clinics and determine the needs of persons requiring social assistance. Provincial administration of services such as these makes possible the variation of levels of service to accord with local priorities. The role of the federal government should be to provide for those transfers of income between people and between provinces which generally support the incomes of people and the services of governments in the different provinces.

The Government of Canada recognizes too that *the provinces should continue to have the constitutional powers required to enable them to embark upon regional economic development programs.* Provincial programs inevitably will affect national policies for economic growth, and vice versa, and the programmes of the several provinces may well be competitive with one another. But the aims and the expectations of people in the several provinces should find expression in provincial as well as federal economic measures. *The provinces must continue, too, to have responsibility for the many intra-provincial matters which call for local rather than national action.*

The Government of Canada holds the view that in the exercise of these responsibilities — which under the present division of powers are at least as wide ranging as those of the federal government — each province should be able to develop its own unique approach. The range of powers we would expect the provinces to have would extend, as they do now, into the areas which are vital to the preservation of Canada's several cultural and regional identities.

We believe, finally, that the provincial governments like the federal government must have taxing powers sufficient to enable them to finance their responsibilities. However, we suspect that in assigning to governments the power of taxation — the capacity for financing public services in Canada — the principle of access to tax powers will supersede the principle of an exact division of tax fields. We would do well to remember that it is as difficult to predict what technological or social or international changes will have increased the role of the provincial or federal governments in 30 years as it would have been to predict the changes between 1938 and 1968.

The fourth generalization we would advance concerning the division of powers has to do with the effect each government's activities inevitably will have upon the activities of the others. This applies both to individual programs and to the totality of government activity. For example, federal income redistribution measures inevitably have an effect upon provincial social welfare programs and provincial resource development policies inevitably affect the rate of growth of the nation's economy. Similarly the aggregate use by the provinces of their spending and borrowing powers inevitably affects federal fiscal, and monetary and balance of payments policies, and the use of the federal spending power affects provincial policies in different ways. Obviously the total volume of spending by each order of government affects the priorities of the other.

We question whether it is any longer realistic to expect that some neat compartmentalization of powers can be found to avoid this. Instead we suspect that the answer is to be found in the processes by which governments consult one another and by which they seek to influence each other before decisions are finally taken. This remedy has been prescribed so often as to appear commonplace. But there is much to be done even in coming to understand the processes of intergovernmental influence, to say nothing of perfecting the machinery by which intergovernmental consultation takes place. Nor will we find the 'participation' of provincial governments in federal government decisions, and vice versa, to be an easy answer to the problems of consultation. The federal government must remain responsible to Parliament, and the provincial governments to their legislatures: federal-provincial conferences must, it seems to us, occupy themselves with the art of influence rather than the power of decision-making.

Both federal and provincial governments will recognize, too, the un-resolved question as to *whether there should be a federal government role when there is a 'national interest' in provincial programs (or the lack of them), or whether there should be a provincial government role when there is a 'provincial interest' in national programs (or the lack of them).* Examples abound: what the provinces do or do not do about urban development unquestionably affects the national interest, and what the federal government does or does not do about tariff policy affects the provincial interest. *We have to consider seriously whether there should be a way for the federal government to seek to influence the provinces in cases where a national interest is involved, and a way for provincial governments to seek to influence the federal government when a provincial interest is involved.*

There are, we think, no easy solutions. What is required is a comprehensive review of the federal-provincial conferences and committees which now exist, how they function, and how their work is co-ordinated. We must be prepared, ‿ seems to the Government of Canada, to give more systematic recognition to these new forms of federalism.

We must be prepared to consider new methods for bringing provincial influence to bear on developing federal policies, and federal influence on developing provincial policies, before decisions have finally been taken. We must be prepared for innovations in the machinery of government which will enable us to preserve the essence of Canada's two great governmental traditions — federalism and parliamentary government.

This text could be subjected to page upon page of analysis. I could round it off with a host of citations from other federal White Papers, but these would add nothing to the basic significance of what has just been read. What, then, does this text tell us? First, it tells us that in any new or revised constitution the central government must hold responsibility for all crucial areas of economic, social, cultural, and political life, that is to say the 'central areas of responsibility essential to the apparatus of the modern sovereign state — economic policy, the equalization of opportunity, technological and cultural development, and international affairs.' It goes without saying, despite the ambiguity in certain expressions used, that 'the modern sovereign state' can only be Canada as a whole, and that the federal government is the government of that 'modern sovereign state.' The White Paper's authors admit nonetheless that 'there are ... of course, areas of responsibility which are shared with the provinces — including cultural matters, regional economic policy, and social security measures,' but the statement merely serves to illustrate their limitations.

From the federal standpoint the provincial governments' role should be complementary to that of the central administration. The province is seen as a regional administrative body rather like a large municipality. 'Most services involving the most immediate contact between the citizen and the government, and those which contribute most directly to the traditions and heritages which are uniquely provincial, should generally be provided by Canada's provincial governments. Strong provincial governments, able to adapt public services to the particular needs of their people, are as essential to meet the facts of diversity in Canada as a strong federal government is to the preservation of Canadian unity.' There it is: we might have expected local services at least to be clearly identified as provincial responsibilities, but no — it is 'most' of them and 'those which contribute most directly to the traditions and heritages which are uniquely provincial' which 'generally' fall to the provinces. So the central government keeps the door open. One will also have noted the employment of expressions such as 'uniquely provincial' to typify the more or less relative importance of provincial attributions. There is to be no exit for the provinces.

The importance of a new and clearer division of powers is minimized in the paper. 'Provincial interests and the interests of Canada's two linguistic groups are not and cannot be represented simply through the device of transferring powers from the federal government to provincial governments.' And farther along, 'the division of powers between orders of government should be guided by principles of functionalism, and not by ethnic considerations.' The provincial acquisition of powers that are currently federal is thus viewed by Ottawa as an expedient: it would be better to rely on 'principles of functionalism,' in other words trust the best-equipped government with the job of discharging a particular responsibility.

As Ottawa, with its resources and the implicit support of the other provinces, is generally better equipped, the federal position as here stated leads logically to an increase in the powers of the federal state. This is the very possibility Ottawa wants to keep open by expressing so functional a principle and so convenient a pragmatism.

The federal text recognizes that 'the governments of the provinces have responsibility for education, and their own power to support technological and cultural development — so often associated with educational institutions.' Would education then be seen by Ottawa as an exclusively provincial jurisdiction? It is not all that certain, for the text also mentions 'an active federal role in the cultural and technological developments which so characterize the 20th century.' Why this 'active role' in an area described as being 'so often associated with educational institutions'? Because 'cultural and technological developments across the country are as essential to nationhood today as tariffs and railways were one hundred years ago.' But tariffs, railways, are exclusively federal. The mere evocation of such a parallel strikes us as highly meaningful, and raises questions of the permanence of an exclusive provincial power in education. What remains to the provinces in terms of health and welfare? There does not seem to be any federal objection to provinces being responsible for hospitals and public health clinics, but Ottawa must preserve 'the rights to make payments to individuals, for the purpose of supporting their income levels — old age security pensions, unemployment insurance, family allowances...'

The White Paper does not place much faith in any so-called watertight division of powers. In this regard it sticks to its 'functional' approach: 'We have to consider seriously whether there should be a way for the federal government to seek to influence the provinces in cases where a national interest is involved, and a way for provincial governments to seek to influence the federal government when a provincial interest is involved.' Mutual influence is to be institutionalized. It is not hard to see where such institutionalization would take us, if we remember that the federal government has always taken it as its prerogative to intervene when, in its opinion, an issue was of 'national interest,' and recall as well that Ottawa's fiscal and financial resources, its spending power, can supply the means to move at any time, and finally if we consider that the other provinces are more inclined to trust Ottawa with some of their present responsibilities than to try taking any away. It will have been noted that nowhere in the text cited is there mention of Quebec. There is no reference of any kind that could allow an outside observer to think the Canadian constitutional problem arose because of Quebec, the province that made discussion on the division of powers the priority.

In short, the White Paper is based on an overall plan with, as its elements, a central government responsible for virtually everything but regional stewardship, and a group of administrative organizations, the provinces. Was the pattern deliberately conceived for the immediate purpose of constitutional negotiation? Does it sum up a starting position that could be altered by circumstance and the tenacity of its antagonists? Does it flow from a dark desire for conquest or is it, despite its apparent candour, the result of a perverse philosophy aimed at the political sterilization of Quebec? The answer in all cases is negative: there is no dark desire, or even bad faith, in the federal theses of this paper or in those, mined from the same vein, found in subsequent documents. Ottawa is quite simply loyal to a solidly-rooted historical tradition, the unmistakable outlines of which could already be discerned in John A. Macdonald's remarks at the time the federation was put together. Suiting its terms to circumstances and times, Ottawa has always been telling us the same thing. The federal government has never ceased to consider itself the government of a country, with all that implies. The only formal distinction in Ottawa's mind between a country of the unitary type and one of the federal variety like Canada is that in the latter, regional governments — those of the provinces — are elected and relatively autonomous in certain areas of local significance, while in the former the regional administrations are set up by the national government. In these instances, however, Ottawa perceives differences only in modalities, no serious difference in kind. The fact that certain Canadian provinces and more specifically Quebec stress the preservation and increase of their autonomy, hence of their powers, is made to look like a freakish anomaly emanating from narrow regionalist thinking and a lack of understanding of the main currents of contemporary change.

Ottawa's error comes of confusing the regionalism of certain provincial administrators, or if you like their narrow-mindedness, with the nationalism of the people of Quebec. For Ottawa, Quebec nationalism is only one variant of the regional loyalty met virtually everywhere in Canada. Never has the idea been seriously entertained in official federal circles that Quebec nationalism springs from a radically different thinking from that nourishing the frequent con- servative spasms of other provinces. My purpose here is not to claim that Quebec delegates to federal-provincial conferences have always displayed imaginativeness and a thinking in advance of the times as against their opposite numbers from other provinces, for such is not the case. Frequently, for example, the Quebec government has opposed Ottawa because it saw 'socialist' tendencies in proposed federal policy, tendencies disrespectful of the private sector.

It is still important to get one thing clear: whatever the vagueness of the arguments of Alexandre Taschereau and Maurice Duplessis, the up-to-date ring of Paul Sauvé's, the wavering resolution of Antonio Barrette's, the dynamism of Jean Lesage's, the subtlety of Daniel Johnson's, the good faith of Jean-Jacques Bertrand's, the federal optimism of Robert Bourassa's, as prime ministers all these individuals have borne unrelenting faith, at least in their official statements, to what might be termed 'a certain idea of Quebec.' And basically, that 'certain idea of Quebec' is no more than the badly expressed and hesitant notion of a 'Quebec that is certain.' In any case it has nothing to do with lingering regionalism. This, however, Ottawa has never understood, and in all probability quite honestly. Like any other living organism, the Canadian federal system can tolerate only a certain amount of internal contradiction: its defence mechanisms will let it go no farther. The regionalism of a province can always be neutralized, since the trend of the modern world will sooner or later scatter on it the seeds of its own demise. But Quebec nationalism, that age-old and instinctive quest for the 'land of Quebec,' has absolutely nothing in common with the elements of the usual federal equation. As a foreign body it is automatically rejected even before it gets very far into the surrounding organism. Officially it is not on the book; something that explains Ottawa's habitual discretion on the Quebec problem in all papers and public statements.

It would be better in terms of federal peace of mind, therefore, to view this nationalism as the aberrant concern of a very limited collection of Quebec intellectuals entrenched here and there in the 'provincial administration,' a few university faculties, and the world of journalism. As for the good people of Quebec, realistic, commonplace, focussed on concrete problems, as certain politicians will tell us, they are not following that microscopic minority of obscure, false prophets in their esoteric lucubrations. There have been fanatics in all countries in all eras: that is all, and it is not that grave, at least according to the Ottawa thesis. During the Quiet Revolution, a number of English-speaking officials in the federal service were persuaded, since the phenomenon emanated from an administration opposed to Duplessis' ideas, that one of its implicit aims was 'to bring Quebec back into Confederation.' For them, Duplessis symbolized Quebec nationalism. Obliged later to face the nationalist fact, they turned to the notion of an unrepresentative 'elite.'

I have already indicated that the federal government has consistently seen itself as the government of a country, but I have yet to bring out one extremely important consequence of that thinking. Beyond my statement's seeming truism lies the desire to consolidate a power whose working could not then be thwarted by inferior administrations. The essence of government is to govern, and Ottawa cannot truly govern if the provinces hold too many exclusive powers or control too many areas where administrative and political action has extensive significance. It will already have been noted, in the federal text analyzed above, that insistence on exclusiveness of powers is slight, while emphasis on mutual influence and functionalism is strong. Let us remember too that the White Paper would place the federal hand on all crucial levers of power. The federal ideal is a unitary Canada: failing that, Ottawa aims as close as it can. Vast areas of administration remain with the provinces, impressive in budgetary terms, fostering the illusion that the provinces taken together have prerogatives that are comparable to Ottawa's. Yet comparison cannot be made in budgetary terms alone. If we try to measure the relative influences of provinces and central government on the orientation and development of our society in all its aspects, we see at once that the division of powers Ottawa wants would confer undisputed leadership on itself. From this standpoint, then, provincial governments are a potential nuisance except when, under federal surveillance, they are busy carrying out local, detailed jobs. The proposals in *Federalism for the Future* aim therefore at making use of this nuisance, since it is politically impossible to eliminate altogether. Again, there is no federal cynicism in this, nothing we might call a plot. The very nature of the federal government impels it to these views.

In somewhat the same sense, the nature of Quebec's government has frequently sent it in search of a true governmental role. Replying in his declaration of 14 September 1966 to the habitual question, 'What does Quebec want?' Daniel Johnson told the Tax Structure Committee: 'As a basis for its nationhood, it [Quebec] wants to be master of its own decision-making in what concerns the human growth of its citizens — that is to say education, social security, and health in all their aspects — their economic affirmation — the power to set up the economic and financial institutions they feel are required — their cultural development — not only the arts and letters, but also the French language — and the Quebec community's external development — its relations with certain countries and international bodies.' To specify the sort of socio-cultural jurisdiction Quebec was looking for, Mr Johnson suggested a redistribution of resources and functions between the orders of government: 'In the terms of the redistribution the government of Quebec would gradually assume sole responsibility in its own territory for all public expenditure relative to education in all forms, old age security, family allowances, health, job placement and manpower training, regional development, and in particular for programs of aid to municipalities, research, and the arts, as well as culture, and generally all services of a socio-cultural nature within our jurisdiction under the present constitution. Existing federal programs in these domains would be taken over by Quebec which, in that event, would preserve their portability.'

The short list cited here includes only those general categories of power Quebec was hoping to attach to its own prerogatives in a new Canadian constitution. Nor have we mentioned the powers that would have remained federal. All these questions gave rise to study after study within the Quebec government. For the purpose of constitutional review, a series of working papers was prepared and made public in October 1968. Among other things they sketched the elements of a new division of powers, and had approval as working documents from the Quebec premier of the day. Here, from these papers, is a partial list of proposed federal powers: defence and the armed forces, foreign policy and diplomatic relations (subject to provincial jurisdiction in the area), the central bank, commercial banks, coinage and exchange rates, customs duties and international trade, international navigation and air transport, regulation of monopolies, the postal service, citizenship, etc. Also provided for were a certain number of shared powers with either federal or provincial paramountcy, such as agriculture, immigration, radio and television broadcasting, and film. Without necessarily being this precise, Jean Lesage, Jean-Jacques Bertrand, and Robert Bourassa have at one time or another expressed views along the same lines as Daniel Johnson's. This holds true if we delve still farther into the past. Quebec's position has always been strongly autonomist.

Between Ottawa's positions as described and those of Quebec, there is a world of difference. Indeed the two are irreconcilable. To make itself a government in the true sense Quebec must also secure some powers now reserved for or exercised by the federal government. If on the other hand Ottawa is really to lead the country, it needs to enlarge its jurisdiction by securing confirmation of powers it has appropriated with or without provincial consent, and officially confirm its general responsibility for the country as a whole, a responsibility tending to establish its unchallengeable superiority over provincial administrations. Major conflict lies in these stands, which themselves arise from basic self-images and tendencies we may qualify as age-old.

No other province has ever held the general political positions of Quebec for the very good reason that none has ever felt the need to do so. Not that they have always been content with their lot in Confederation; on the contrary, their grievances have been and continue numerous. Basically, however, their implications have never gone beyond the realms of administration or finance. With very rare exceptions, Quebec's positions have always gone hand in hand with assertions of principle which have frequently irritated representatives of other governments but which made it quite clear that Quebec defined itself as an autonomous territory desiring to become more so, while the powers of its government were regularly menaced by Ottawa-based invasion. Behind all this lies the historical fact that the government in Quebec City is senior to the one in Ottawa. In this sense, the federal government may be viewed as the creature of those provinces originally joining in Confederation, an argument sometimes used by Quebec public men to prove that it is not the Quebec government's part to do homage to Ottawa. At the same time, the federal government stands at the origin of the provinces in the west, and this federal origin is much more recent than the social development and improvement of the territory where Quebec now is: Alberta and Saskatchewan have only enjoyed provincial status, and this by federal law, since 1905. Thus, one can understand why there are two ways of seeing the federal government in Canada: some see it as instituted by the provinces, while for others the contrary is the case. It is only very rarely that one of the English-speaking 'founding' provinces advances the argument of seniority: Ontario is virtually the only one ever to have done so. Quebec, however, is much more attached to the idea, an attitude explained by settlement much more venerable than in any other province, 'founding' or otherwise. 'Quebeckers' have been along the St Lawrence now for over three centuries and a half.

The relation between Ottawa and the provinces is not viewed in anything like the same way by the Quebecker, the Ontarian, the Newfoundlander, or the citizen of Saskatchewan or British Columbia. For most Quebeckers, Ottawa holds no authority over the government of Quebec, as Quebec does not over the federal administration. Each is autonomous in its proper jurisdiction. Sometimes their actions are complementary. If conflict arises, the right is *a priori* with Quebec City. For Quebeckers, moreover, the federal government is traditionally English-speaking and given to recurrent bouts of intrigue for the arrogation of prerogatives beyond its own. Obviously we could add subtlety to this crude delineation of current Quebec sentiment, for the view can vary with the citizen's social and geographical situation. Nevertheless it has long been and at present continues to be a common denominator of Quebec opinion.

The common denominator in other provinces is the equation of 'federal' with 'national' government. Neither Newfoundlander nor British Columbian would cast doubt on this fundamental. Having established it, they may certainly go on to complain that their 'national' government is neglecting them or failing to understand their regional difficulties. If serious conflict arises between provincial and 'national' government, however, there is no guarantee at all that the citizen's sympathy will flow towards the government of his province. All public men in these English-speaking provinces agree that it is up to Ottawa to set the country's general course, establish 'national' standards, in short exercise all the authority normally expected of the government of a country, providing only that it does not unduly disturb current provincial programs. From time to time we hear their voices raised against what Ottawa is doing, and there may even be talk of federal invasion of provincial prerogative that sounds a little like Quebec's. Yet these protests have not the same scope, or even the same sense. Moreover they are often based on electoral concerns, occasionally in the dubious company of plans for political revenge; they may as easily express conservative reaction. Certainly Quebec politics have known similar motivation, but friction between Ottawa and the English-speaking provinces almost never arises from the feeling that the federal authorities are menacing provincial integrity.

In English-speaking Canada, the Ottawa-province relation is frequently one of superior to inferior. It is seen as such by Ottawa as well as those provinces. A provincial minister, even a premier, seems to have received a promotion if he goes into the federal Cabinet. No longer is a Quebec politician necessarily 'promoted' on moving from the Quebec to the Ottawa arena: the two are comparable. Yet for federal people, elected representatives and civil servants, the 'provincials' do not call for much respect, fixed as they are, or as Ottawa assumes them to be, on the short term, and given to material administrative concerns. We might ask ourselves, in fact, whether being a 'provincial politician' does not tend to bring with it a narrowing of the political horizon, since the 'provincial' is, so to speak, condemned to administer the present, while it is lawful and natural for the 'federal' to lay the groundwork of the future. If this occupational characteristic is a genuine one, and I believe it to be, the consequences for the Quebec government are grave. It is a vicious circle: the provincial politician is more given to current and immediate policies than is his federal colleague and, particularly if there is an absence of general policies, ends up an administrative waterboy, all the time on the go, an activity which, draining as it is, may ultimately emerge as an excuse for the want of overall policy.

The federal 'gospel' from which I have been citing a few verses corresponds in every particular to Anglo-Canadian opinion of the prerogatives and powers of a 'national' government. No public man in any English-speaking province, whatever his party allegiance, has ever cast doubt on these prerogatives and powers. It was obvious during the ill-fated process of constitutional review that all English Canada concurred with the stated federal position. In other words, the majority of Canada's citizens felt at one with Ottawa and saw in its position ideas and principles that struck them as axiomatic. Just as obviously, Quebec was not of this camp, and in the minds of the other provinces Quebec's stand amounted to an assault on the very basis of the federal system as they and their people understood it. This meant that in order to satisfy Quebec, the constitutional review would have had to convince the rest of Canada to give up its concept of the country and the central government. And to succeed in the negotiations on the division of powers, preserve the prerogatives of its government, conclude certain questions in limbo, Quebec will have to keep persisting and persist forever in the hope of shifting the rest of the country's opinion on the nature of Canada and the powers that should naturally fall to the central administration.

Mission impossible? Truly, yet no one can blame the English-Canadian majority for wanting their 'national' government to give the country genuine leadership. It would be absurd to require English Canadians to adopt an idea of the federal government similar to the one Quebeckers have had. It would be asking them to act against their own natures. But if English Canada does not want to see the federal government in relation to itself otherwise than it has done up to now, would it at least agree that the Quebec-Ottawa relation is essentially different from the Ontario-Ottawa or Alberta-Ottawa relation? Without changing the system, which would require a prior change in thinking, whether out of fear of Quebec or for any other reason, the answer is negative. For sociological, historical, and political reasons the rest of the country tends to the belief that the concept of the federal government that goes for Ontario, Saskatchewan, or Prince Edward Island also has to suit that 'other' province of Quebec.

12
Fellow Travellers:
The Conference Room

It is often said that when discussion enters the realm of principle it is virtually doomed to failure, however slight the warring parties' devotion to their own ideas. Sincere federalists are not surprised and even less shocked to note that Ottawa's and Quebec's basic political approaches are fundamentally divergent. For them this situation is quite natural, and it would be naïve to get upset over it. The best thing is to set principles aside, with the confrontations they involve, and instead take a pragmatic line, using, for example, the possibilities of intergovernmental co-operation.

The Duplessis régime was much criticized for its negative attitudes towards Ottawa and for abetting Quebec's withdrawal into itself. Coming to office in 1960, Jean Lesage adopted a policy of openness, and at the first federal-provincial conference in which he participated, in July 1960, proposed the creation of a permanent federal-provincial secretariat. There was never formal acceptance for the secretariat Lesage proposed. Other provinces feared the entrenchment of intergovernmental technocracy, probably expensive and certainly powerful. Reiterated by Daniel Johnson and Jean-Jacques Bertrand, the suggestion never won more than a polite expression of interest. Ottawa did not turn it down, but was not particularly anxious to see it installed, since the federal government already had all the necessary personnel and could easily mobilize them to make the material arrangements for conferences: only adequate premises were lacking. In any case Ottawa could not see how such an institution could emanate from the shared desire of 11 governments. It seemed preferable that if such a secretariat were ever set up it should be in the wake of a federal decision accepted by the provincial administrations. As for staff, though it could have included officials seconded by provinces, Ottawa thought it more normal that they should be attached to the federal civil service and occupy a building supplied by Ottawa. Here is evidence of the federal government's concept of its

role in these relations: Ottawa must maintain the initiative and co-ordinate relations, and thus Ottawa must supply, without ruling out a degree of provincial participation, most of the personnel and services eventually required.

At the time the constitutional review was getting under way in 1968, a secretariat for the conference was set up in compliance with these federal 'norms.' It nonetheless meant a definite improvement in the process. When the review was put on ice in 1971, a new role had to be devised for this office. At the federal-provincial premiers' conference in November of that year, the suggestion was made that it be confirmed, notably by a change in title, in the role it had gradually been assuming since 1969-70, when it began to get involved in federal-provincial meetings on subjects other than the constitution, a development no one had objected to at the time. The decision was put off, however, to another day.

The proposal had come from Ottawa and taken the form of a working document emanating from the secretariat itself. For several years, in fact, Ottawa had been thinking of setting up an organization in the capital to deal with the various federal-provincial meetings. Without openly advancing the idea, it did remodel the old Union Station as a 'conference centre,' in accordance with a plan known to a number of provincial officials for a long time. There the conference secretariat had been installed. Quebec's most serious reservation on the federal proposal emerged at the November 1971 conference not in terms of basics, that is the potential dependence of such an agency on Ottawa, but in terms of form. If the name were changed to something like 'secretariat of federal-provincial relations' we were admitting, Quebec feared, the demise of constitutional review. The gesture would have been politically dangerous in the fall of 1971, being in at least seeming contradiction with Prime Minister Bourassa's statements to the effect that the review would continue despite the Victoria setback, In any event, without being formally abolished, the secretariat was dismantled for all practical purposes a few months later, in January 1972. Ontario protested: Quebec lay low, though it had led the way a dozen years previously in calling for such a body. Today Ottawa is running no more risks: it is taken for granted that the federal administration is directly and solely responsible for maintaining that conspicuous function of the Canadian system that, with time, federal-provincial gatherings have become.

Are federal-provincial conferences, as frequent and sometimes clamorous as they are, really a help to co-operation among the various governments? The classic reply is this: even if the system is still imperfect, federal-provincial meetings do give governments a practical opportunity to work out their policies together, apart from differences in principle, to consult before acting, co-ordinate decisions and acts. Moreover each government leaves with a better understanding of the others' positions, and more clearly recognizes the difficulties and special conditions that may have to be faced in other parts of Canada. Those supporting this idea may admit the meetings can occasion some fairly acid exchanges, but attribute these in a general way to frictions natural and inevitable in any federal system. If there are tensions and conflicts, they see their cause as lying in misunderstandings that further consultation might give us a chance to allay. In short, they conclude, federal-provincial conferences in Canada are developing as a forum for airing government policy. These conferences have gradually assumed such importance that we could no longer do without them. At the intergovernmental level, they evidence the new spirit of participation any healthy democracy must foster in the whole of its constituency.

This reply is certainly not without truth. It has been dished up so often it may now be seen as a 'received' idea, and I cavil at the risk of seeming picayune. However, we must penetrate beyond this superficial and incomplete interpretation in order to be capable of evaluating what a political hatchet for Ottawa the federal-provincial conferences have become. It is only through experiencing several of them that one begins to see their potential power, the usefulness of which Ottawa has grasped better in the past few years.

Taken as a group, the provinces generally frame two criticisms of the consultation system, though one is not always certain whether they are aimed at the conference mechanism or the federal attitude. Whichever the case, it must be admitted that these criticisms, often dictated by provincial politics, are based on a more or less intentional non-comprehension of the results that can normally be expected of intergovernmental discussion. For this reason they should be disposed of at once.

When, during such a conference or in its wake, Ottawa announces a policy which appeared on the agenda, there is always at least one province to claim no true consultation took place because the federal authorities did not accept provincial suggestions. The criticism does not stand up. For one thing, provincial suggestions are often improvised. Even based on the same study, they may contradict suggestions from other provinces. How could Ottawa pick up both? Some provinces confidently expect that if they express any opinion Ottawa must take it into consideration. Their view may in fact be absolutely pertinent, but that is not the issue. Consultation does not mean that one party commits himself to use all opinions the other is good enough to give him. The consultation-acceptance equation is a false one. If no provincial proposal were ever accepted by Ottawa, of course, there would be just reason for complaint. There has even, and frequently, been a total lack of intergovernmental consultation, an omission pointed out sometimes vehemently by all provinces,

Quebec included. But for Ottawa to reject suggestions on occasion is perfectly natural.

The second criticism is aimed at the apparent lack of tangible results, and for 'tangible' read 'financial,' of some federal-provincial meetings. This criticism is no more penetrating than the other. Some provinces reason as if the federal government should compensate them each time for their presence in Ottawa, so to speak, by paying increased conditional grants or enlarging tax areas in their favour. Ottawa may well refuse fiscal or financial transfers for wrong or clearly unacceptable reasons. Given this, however, the rules of the present system do not oblige the federal authorities to hand out lollipops to every province vouchsafing a delegation.

We can now move on to more apposite considerations on Ottawa's use of the conference mechanism. The multiplicity of intergovernmental meetings over the past few years is not especially the result of sudden conversion to the benefits of consultation in the federal quarter, or the implementation of what might be termed a 'policy of participation' for the provinces. Nor does it arise from any wish to decentralize the decision-making process. The frequency of these encounters is really a consequence of the fact that Ottawa is working out 'national' policies that can only be implemented by provincial governments or bodies they control. If Ottawa plans a move into their jurisdiction it must manage to 'mobilize' the provinces. Intergovernmental meetings are one means of conditioning them to this action. How, for example, could Ottawa set up a cross-Canada health insurance scheme if the provinces declined to co-operate? The program would run up against enormous constitutional difficulties. It is better for Ottawa to skirt the issue, waiting for the right moment or even arranging it, at the risk of having to prove that the proposed program fills a need, the people are depending on it, and at all events, some provinces have already signalled acceptance. Even if, as was the case exactly with medicare, most provinces are initially hostile to an idea, the central spending power combined with conference conditioning will almost always let Ottawa reach its objective sooner or later. The same thinking applies to such measures as vocational training, regional development, social assistance, and so on. One might say that the incidence of federal-provincial conferring rises proportionately as Ottawa wants to get involved in areas that lie beyond its own jurisdiction. Once involved, there is no retreating: in 1968-9, federal representatives were admitting Ottawa had moved on medicare without adequate consultation, and might even have infringed provincial prerogative, but the move had been made and there was an election promise at stake. (Quebec, incidentally, which did not go into medicare straight away, was never repaid the $200 million its citizens sent to Ottawa in Social Development Tax to finance it.) Even when Ottawa wants to make some new move within its own jurisdiction, it needs support from the provinces, if only to ensure they will not do anything liable to run counter to federal policy.

Ottawa may also be feeling the need to ignite the public imagination by presenting new plans in an alluring light. Though they are not the only way of doing so, or even necessarily the most effective way, federal-provincial conferences do provide a convenient political stage. For this reason television cameras appeared at the December 1967 housing conference. The innovation was undoubtedly prompted by the televising of the Ontario-sponsored Confederation of Tomorrow Conference in the previous month. Perhaps Ottawa did not want to be left out. In any case, four or five federal ministers were able to tell the Canadian public about what had already been achieved, and the central régime's bountiful intentions in so vital a sector. The fact that the audience for the broadcasts was fairly sparse does nothing to change the aim of the publicity. Cases of this kind have been reasonably infrequent, however, and after that only the constitutional conferences were seen on television.

Cameras or no cameras, federal-provincial conferences on any topic always spawn their quota of news stories. The propaganda that can come out of them would not be enough on its own to justify holding the meetings, but it is by no means negligible as a background factor. The provinces too can take advantage of these opportunities, and do not scruple to do so. On the whole, however, the federal government has the trumps. First, Ottawa announces the agenda and sets the tone. Ottawa also invites the journalists of the federal press gallery, representing information media that cover all of Canada, to preliminary press conferences informing them of the cogency of the proposals to be set before the provinces. As the federal minister or prime minister chairs not only the Ottawa delegation but the meeting itself, it is inevitable that he be asked to sum the conference up when it concludes: hence, another news report that sends the federal message across the country. More often than not, the final press communiqué originates with the federal group. Dissatisfied provincial participants must then try to correct it. During the entire conference the chief Canadian representative has invariably been interviewed as he leaves the sessions. His words, whatever they are, will no doubt be reported by television, radio, the papers, but the same is not necessarily true for the provincial people, whose comments are very often inspired by local concerns of small interest to the rest of the country, and lack what the journalist's jargon characterizes as 'national interest.'

The same holds true for briefs and studies from participating governments. Ottawa's are assured of wide diffusion, the provinces' of much less. If a province wants more publicity, it can always invite journalists to a press conference, but it is assumed that the information will have no public comparable to the one Ottawa reaches every day through its press gallery. We may also mention that, even if they wanted to, the reporters could not give equal prominence to federal and provincial statements, with one federal government and ten provincial: that is a lot of people.

As far as publicity goes, Quebec's position is relatively better than that of other provinces. The space given its views is always greater. Reporters expect a stand contradicting Ottawa's, an element of assured news value. The chairman of the Quebec delegation is always more in demand for comment than his colleagues from other provinces. Quebec papers often give him coverage equal to or better than the coverage given the federal leader. (The same occurs in their home provinces, though much less often, for leaders of other provincial delegations.) Outside Quebec, the Quebec positions are covered, but the prevailing tendency is to stress their negative relation to the federal stand.

On the whole, the thing to remember is that Ottawa talks to the entire country during such conferences, while provincial representatives run the risk of reaching only their own constituents. That is to be expected, people will say, since the federal government is the government of the whole country, while provinces have only a limited territorial influence. This reply omits to take into account one appreciable factor, however: Ottawa is quite capable of taking advantage of its privileged situation, and indeed does so, to extol its own achievements and present policies affecting areas beyond its jurisdiction, encouraging in the population and above all the English-speaking population a desire for increased federal presence. By this means and others at its command Ottawa may win currency for the idea that Canadians must turn to it if they want benefit from the broad 'national' policies. It does not matter whether the domains affected by them are federal or provincial.

Though the system is well broken in, it is by no means free from bugs. Coverage, thought excessive by some, may focus on well-grounded provincial reservations, or worse still, grave misunderstandings. These setbacks are only momentary, however, since the credibility of overstubborn provinces, Quebec's in particular, finally wears thin. Those following the federal-provincial debates more or less attentively can be left with the impression that 'the provinces are never satisfied.' It does appear, moreover, that provinces more and more have the name without the game. In the early 1960s, provinces, though almost never successful in getting Ottawa to abandon any project to which it was firmly attached, did at least manage to exert a material influence on federal policy. This is no longer the case. Ottawa has learned by experience, and now, when a conference opens, we can often assume that calling it was the last formality before implementation of the policies that are supposed to be under discussion and not by any means the first, as those people tend to believe who think Ottawa's anxiety for consultation is genuine. All that remains is to secure support from the provincial rank and file and check a few technical details. Ottawa never summons a conference without certainty of ultimate success, even taking into account the delays some provincial reservations may entail. For Ottawa, in contrast to the naive assumption of some onlookers that failure or success are written in the final conference statements or the innuendos of the official communiqué, the happy conclusion may quite easily arrive six months, a year, or even longer afterwards.

The present federal-provincial conference system gives Ottawa another trump that tends to be overlooked. It almost always has the initiative. With its financial resources and its competent and abundant civil service personnel Ottawa can have policies and programs all worked out for presentation to the provinces as the occasion arises. Ottawa may even make helpful suggestions on subjects of provincial prerogative. Taking the chair, it plays two roles, leader and participant. As chairman, Ottawa gives the floor to one province or another and introduces the subjects to be discussed; as participant it replies to objections raised, furnishes added details, and so forth. Ottawa is in fact the kingpin of these conferences. It is perfectly obvious that the situation works in its favour. Moreover, in the vast majority of cases Ottawa provides the conference venue as well. Federal representatives have all their files and officials on the spot, a proximity of resources that sometimes means a distinct advantage. Ottawa is further responsible for drawing up the agenda. This is clearly done with provincial suggestions in mind, but the central government is the final arbiter as far as arrangement and relative emphasis of questions are concerned. The consultation leading up to the conference itself enables Ottawa to form a fairly definite idea of possible provincial reaction to the suggestions it is preparing to throw in. Though provinces are not without resources of their own in this regard, none can rely on so specific and comprehensive a fund of information. And there is nothing to stop the federal government from discreetly soliciting support from likely provinces before the meetings open.

Ottawa's preponderance in the Canadian system of intergovernmental relations has never really come under attack. Some provinces, Quebec included, have raised criticism, but without ever carrying it very far. The fact is that we soon run up against necessity: someone has to be responsible for the progress of federal-provincial relations, and a first glance reveals no major reason for refusing the role to the government of the country. In so doing, however, we give that government substantial authority which it can wield with adroitness, as it has in fact done, to extract the maximum possible advantage from the situation. In the preceding chapter, I noted that provinces other than Quebec quite readily accept this implicit federal authority as a natural result of the central government's leadership in the country as a whole. We can be sure that if Quebec were to suggest modifying the current practice by, for instance, rotating the chair or choosing chairmen from outside federal and provincial circles, it would get no real support from any other government in Canada. In the circumstances, short of boycotting all intergovernmental meetings, Quebec can only go along with the system. It is a system that gives rise to considerable political difficulty for Quebec. The rules have been evolved gradually as if the central government were the natural leader in all things of ten regional administrative structures. Now Quebec is unhappy in a situation that in practice denies its true dimension. With its attitude frequently inspired by a thinking divergent from that of Ottawa and other provinces, Quebec must not only use effort in argument that others do not have to expend, but must also labour to neutralize the intrinsic disadvantages of the system.

Could Quebec still do more to make use of the resources of interprovincial co-operation? Let us see. According to the second Lesage proposal in 1960: 'This area of interdependence has been misconstrued for too long. The provinces have more and more common problems among themselves, which they could surely examine together and perhaps also, one must hope, solve together.' One after another, Quebec's leaders have soon learned from experience how deceptive it is to hope to convert the federal government to their views in intergovernmental encounters. Arriving in office, they always suffer from what might be called a 'crisis of good faith' — the belief, lasting six months to a year, that they will succeed where others have bitten the dust, that with them federalism will bear fruit, that Ottawa will yield to their desires. Each in turn tries new tactics: broad negotiation, ad hoc discussion, enlightened pragmatism, reliance on unassailable principle, firmness, obstinacy, sweetness, suppleness, acerbity, prudent silence, and so on. Not one of these tactics ever genuinely contributed to solving the basic Quebec problem. The agenda of dispute is longer today than the one we were grappling with a decade ago.

Since no premier or minister in Quebec has been or is now an independentist, none has dared either to reject the system outlined here or to openly recognize that in the present state of affairs Ottawa has no intention of solving the problems the system spawns. These politicians are caught in a mesh that obliges them to their more or less conditional federal allegiance. Challenging this would shatter the very foundations of their allegiance. They have to grin and bear it, looking elsewhere for solutions to the malaise they feel as Quebec public men.

One classic recipe for grinning in the circumstances is to periodically rediscover and display the supposedly numerous virtues of interprovincial co-operation. If Quebec cannot succeed with Ottawa on its own, they tell themselves, it can do so with support from other provinces. The basic hypothesis is that Ottawa, facing a phalanx of provinces around the Quebec standard, will have no alternative but to cave in. So they peacefully confect the notion that if Quebec does not enjoy more success in persuading Ottawa, the cause lies not in a new round of federal incomprehension but rather in the absence of enough solidarity from other provinces, cast by this means as the inadvertent 'bad guys' of a conveniently false scenario. Ottawa's not guilty plea is reinforced, and there will be no need to cast doubt on the federal system as such.

The quest for a provincial common front elicits one statement after another and raises many hopes in Quebec. Sidestepping the problem, it also avoids a number of disquieting questions as to Ottawa's innate attitude to provinces in general and Quebec in particular. But this famous common front, in the sense in which we understand the term, is a myth. It has always been a myth, at least during the past ten or twenty years, but each new government in Quebec City has gone to it as a more or less willing sacrifice. They persist in thinking it is possible because as soon as two, three, or even all ten provinces evince similar points of view, certain provincial conferees, and especially conference observers, hasten to depict a common and permanent desire to resist federal encroachment. These people never specify how long such desires have previously managed to last, or even if they have ever modified Ottawa's view of the situation. At most we may cite minor alterations in federal planning, something Ottawa can use to say it has taken provincial advice into consideration.

In fact there is only one set of circumstances in which, to all appearances, a common front exists. As soon as financial resources arrive on the agenda, all provinces, even without prior consultation, agree that the federal government has too much in relation to their own. The attitude is so predictable that the first analyst on the spot when a fiscal conference is announced can state with certainty that the provinces will band together to grab all they can get from Ottawa. But is this really a common front? No, unless the words have lost their normal meaning. Apart from the immediate objective or natural reflex of wanting to extract a larger share of federal funds, provincial inclinations towards concerted action, even in the hypothetical case that these inclinations were produced by rational group decision, would melt away as soon as it came to the forms of transfer. One province, Quebec, wants more fiscal latitude and more equalization. Another, British Columbia for example, would reject equalization, which brings nothing to the Pacific, and ask only for a fiscal enlargement, while yet another, let us say Nova Scotia or perhaps Newfoundland, would definitely prefer the equalization, more profitable in its own case than fiscal extension. In a word, agreement on the capital problem of determining how a resource transfer can be accomplished, even supposing Ottawa consented to it, is virtually non-existent. Often Ottawa has no need to render itself loathsome by categorical refusal: the provinces themselves take the responsibility of making the transfer impracticable, or showing that if it occurred it would not satisfy everybody.

This is a curious sort of common front, yet it is persistently conjured up to show the potential power of interprovincial co-operation. Those in Quebec who count heavily on increased and constant interprovincial co-operation are generally making two mistakes. The first is to imagine that all provinces have similar problems and if they are prodded a little, similar reactions to Ottawa's potential role in solving them. In other words, they believe that what is good for one province has chances of being good for another, since it too is a province: as if natural resources, demography, local institutions, and culture could keep company with the political status of a state. That comparable situations are to be found in Quebec, Ontario, and Saskatchewan no one will deny, but it is wrong to claim on that basis that these three provinces will want to confront the problems in the same way, and take the same approach with Ottawa. The truth is otherwise, and here we are touching on the second mistake made by certain Quebec advocates of interprovincial co-operation. Nuances exist in the concept of central government from one province to another, but Quebec's view differs substantially from those of all other provinces taken together. For them, as we know, the federal is the 'senior' government from which one awaits aid and favour; one does not attempt fundamental debate of its activity and role, even while complaining as do the western provinces, that its bounty is not up to its estimated capability. There is never any question of setting at it thoroughly, attacking it more fiercely than is fitting or than provincial voters can accept.

A common front calls for three basic elements. Two of these, identical views of a problem and an organized strategy to combat it, are unsatisfied now and likely to remain so when Quebec is after a permanent increase in autonomy and not simply ad hoc accommodations. The third is the presence, if not of an 'enemy,' at least of an obstacle to be faced together. Now the English-speaking provinces see no obstacle in Ottawa, no dangerously centripetal administration. More than anything else they see a government that is big, powerful, and rich, that must not be put in a temper and from which one can sometimes, with luck and electoral clout, extract benefits and contributions. In these circumstances any desire for a coherent and lasting common front is a piece of political utopianism.

With all this in mind we can better understand why in 1960, when the first interprovincial conference for more than a generation convened, English-speaking provinces wanted Quebec's assurance that the move was not going to lead to what at the time they called 'ganging up,' a provincial conspiracy against Ottawa. With this proviso, they accepted Quebec's invitation, although they even asked and obtained that federal observers be at the meeting. Since then, organizers have generally tried to exclude from the agenda any topic liable to be offensive to Ottawa. Reasonably argumentative issues do arise from time to time, of course, but their appearance is more or less accidental. In fact, by deciding to stick to interprovincial questions, the premiers' conference lost one of its major potential attractions. The topics discussed do nothing to pry more money out of the federal purse. For this reason, participants in the conference are not all that interested in coming or taking the trouble to prepare. Not all provincial premiers attend with regularity. The result is that the year's conference bears so little fruit, beyond a few statements of principle and some publicity, that its purpose is often questioned even by the premiers themselves. Moreover when the annual gathering was started in 1960, federal-provincial conferences, occasions when provincial ministers could meet, were a good deal less frequent than they have since become.

Despite everything, provincial officials telephone around each July to find agenda items that will not seem too contrived. These efforts are virtually preceded by the rationale: this interprovincial conference does not aim at solving problems, but rather gives the premiers a chance to improve acquaintance and discuss their affairs informally in an atmosphere of relaxation. Ontario and Quebec have taken the meeting more seriously, and have at least attempted to raise the great issues of the day, as for instance new trends in government or the fight against pollution. Their success has been mitigated, as most premiers are little inclined in mid-summer — the conference occurs in early August, and amid the relaxation already cited — to attack anything of size, especially in the absence of Ottawa, the big spender. Unanimous resolutions have wended their way to that capital from time to time, asking for delay or change in federal action, or, as was the case from Halifax in 1972 in urban affairs, far from asking Ottawa to vacate the provincial areas it was getting into, the provincial conference told the federal people how to proceed so as not to disturb provincial jurisdiction too much. The resolutions have made little impression on their recipients in the federal Cabinet, but they have had the advantage of proving to the public that the meetings were not totally unproductive. Like other interprovincial resolutions, those from Halifax have gone almost without practical result.

Ottawa really has no reason to fear a potential common front, a vigorous and staunch movement among the provinces. As any even slightly lucid and realistic government in Quebec ought to be, the federal authority is perfectly well aware that interprovincial co-operation can at present do nothing more than stick to bilateral arrangements, generally of a technical nature, or exert momentary pressure on the central power. It must be stressed that those provinces differing with Quebec in such circumstances have in no sense the impression of betraying their interests or the confidence of a member of the circle. As they see it, Quebec is outside the group, detaching itself time and time again by its attitude. They do not feel bound to show any particular loyalty to Quebec. We should also recall at this point that they view the Ottawa-province relation differently: alliance with Ottawa, even against Quebec, has no reprehensible connotation, nor does acting as Ottawa's indirect spokesman. From their own viewpoint, they are undoubtedly right: they were born provinces and largely subject to federal rule; they intend to remain so, and, in contrast to Quebec, leave unchallenged what they see as a natural pattern of Canada's political life. Interprovincial co-operation is therefore neither the imagined arena for Quebec to promote its views nor the lifebuoy of a renewed federalism. The provinces, including Quebec on occasion, are not unaware that they can better find immediate profit in advantageous bilateral arrangements with Ottawa than by instigating a concerted action at the provincial level.

13
The Fifth Column, and the Sixth

Since its position on division of powers and the nature of Canadian federalism is clearly irreconcilable with Ottawa's and lacks support from other provinces in the country, how far can Quebec's government rely on Quebec members in the federal Parliament to press its case and increase its political autonomy?

The responsibility for publication of Quebec views falls primarily, of course, on the government itself. For this purpose the classic tool is the brief, a document made public in federal-provincial discussion. The Quebec briefs are all part of a process, helping to define one another and adding up, in the long run, to an official opus of political documentation. The questions dealt with are often immediate ones, but the briefs rarely lack statements of the principles guiding the government in defining its concept of Canadian federalism. Under all administrations, we have stuck to these principles, and together they constitute a sort of ideal which, from conference to conference, we look for means of realizing. They also evidence a basic continuity, even though they may be expressed in varying terms from one era to another. Besides the official briefs, of course, numerous ministerial speeches and official statements make Quebec's position known, and exchanges of views in the federal-provincial gatherings themselves supply Quebec's interlocutors with further details on government thinking.

This self-presentation procedure is far from infallible, and Quebec periodically feels the need to look to other methods of persuasion. We have already seen that support, except in terms of immediate material advantage from Ottawa, is hard to find among the other Canadian provinces; in this realm the disinterested gesture is unknown. The distinction must always be made between the occasional measure of support for more intensive exploitation of federal sources under existing programs, and the impossibility of such support for Quebec's underlying aim of changing the country's basic organization. The same distinction is useful in deciding the extent to which Quebec's federal MPs and Quebeckers working as high Ottawa officials can help Quebec. Especially since 1970, much has been made of the positive and active understanding we could expect from this sort of 'fifth column' in Ottawa. Supporters of the idea argued as if the presence in Pierre Elliott Trudeau's team of a number of prestigious ministers of Quebec origin, beginning with the Canadian prime minister himself, meant that Quebec could rely as never before on federal interlocutors who would support its positions and gain their acceptance in the federal administration and the rest of Canada.

To acquire a real understanding of the influence of Quebec politicians and civil servants working in the federal government of Canada, it is absolutely essential to remember that these people must develop within a given administrative framework, with existing procedures, customs, priorities, and concerns that are not necessarily aligned with Quebec objectives. Nor can we forget that these politicians and officials are not alone in Ottawa: with them, and there well before them, is an entire staff on which they must rely and who are themselves not necessarily Quebec oriented. At the same time, we will not succumb to the facile, superficial criticism that in spite of all their efforts Quebeckers will never manage to take over the immense federal machine, but will be swallowed up by it instead. Certainly, Quebeckers may be its more or less easy victims: this has frequently occurred and will continue to occur. But it is wrong to claim on this basis, as if from firm evidence, that they cannot now and never will be able to control, even momentarily, the structure and policy of the Ottawa government. On the contrary, they can do so, either in Cabinet or in strategic official posts. This was in fact almost the case, at least as concerned politicians, with the advent of the Trudeau régime. Never before had so many French-speaking Quebeckers been in a position to wield such decisive influence on the central administration of Canada.

Yet how much confidence could Quebec really place in this immense 'fifth column'? Besides their action in favour of bilingualism, taken partly as a sort of separatism insurance, these Quebeckers certainly did everything in their power to secure all possible benefit for Quebec from the federal programs in force. There were two main categories here: the programs already operating by definite standards, and those giving ministers and officials greater freedom in terms of amounts allocated to any particular province. In the case of the first, it was very hard for anyone in Ottawa to find new and unexpected bounty for Quebec; Quebec was either able to enjoy the advantages of these programs under existing criteria or else did not meet the criteria and could not, whatever the good will of the architects of 'French Power,' qualify as the target of federal largesse. With programs of variable financial impact, the latitude enjoyed by the administration could allow instances of munificence to Quebec, and it goes without saying that there was a general disposition to keep Quebec City adequately informed of all advantages to be expected from current and new federal policies.

Was it possible, though, with 'French Power,' to reorient the whole of the central government's economic and social policy in favour of Quebec? Here is where we have to take into account the counterweight of the rest of Canada. A 'pro-Quebec' Ottawa administration could certainly not operate without restriction: not only was it extremely problematical to win acceptance in other provinces and the various federal services for a major shift in Ottawa policy, but it could also be predicted that this administration would find itself unable even to place any special emphasis on rectifying past oversights. Any federal administration wanting to help Quebec would have to do so within the parameters allowed by the rest of the country. As it happens, the opening is so narrow that anything but more or less temporary financial benefit passes with difficulty. And even in this case, as experience has shown us, our Ottawa compatriots can manage to get English Canada's back up, and must then face the consequences at the polls. A federal administration that is over-solicitous towards Quebec is soon suspect in English-Canadian opinion. Nothing spectacular is needed; it is enough merely to seem to favour Quebec, something that occurs, for instance, when Quebec federal ministers stand up for their own political ends to emphasize the tangible interest they bear their home province and the financial advantages federalism has to offer. Unless we assume that until these ministers reached Ottawa the central power had openly and deliberately deprived Quebec of payments due by right, and assume further that the rest of Canada was moved to repentance by this situation, we have to conclude that these ministers are incapable of instigating so profound a reorientation in federal expenditure as to pay out several hundreds of millions of dollars Quebec would not otherwise have received. It is even harder for those Quebeckers in the Cabinet to get substantial modifications in broad federal policies affecting, for instance, agriculture, energy, and transport. There is too much at stake in the rest of Canada. The difference between a federal government totally dominated by the Anglo-Saxon element, which has almost always been the case, and one strongly influenced by French-speaking Quebeckers, which came about with the arrival of the Trudeau team, can thus at best express itself in cultural terms by greater insistence on respect for French language rights and in financial terms by a few more tens of millions of dollars over a limited period.

A government's budgetary freedom is much less than is often believed. Unless its aims are genuinely revolutionary, any administration has to have a fairly long time to set its own stamp on governmental priorities. In other words, it is not easy to whisk really large amounts off to new destinations; most of the time, they are already committed. Budgetary constraint is such that the government has, as we have noted, only a few millions to play with. The political jingling of these millions will, however, be amplified in Quebec's case by official loudspeakers so that the public may be led to believe themselves the blithe recipients of enormous sums that would never have reached them without the vital presence in Ottawa of pro-Quebec elements who are determined to remedy past practices discriminating against Quebec, or at least not discriminating in Quebec's favour. Anticipating a bumper financial harvest from the Trudeau government in Ottawa, the Bourassa government taking office in April 1970 saw the short-term philosophy of 'paying' federalism as a sure thing. The new administration was convinced that the friendly relations between politicians in the two capitals would yield vast new benefits. Bourassa was hoping to use them to prove how disastrous Quebec independence would be, since the federal spring would automatically dry up. He also wanted to show how right Quebeckers were in electing a team determined to avoid pointless conflict with the central power. In reality, however, the fruits of 'paying' federalism turned out to be less abundant than genuinely had been expected, and during the spring of 1972 we saw several key members of the Quebec Cabinet in rebellion against some of the side-effects of this type of federalism — more and more obvious Ottawa incursions into a host of provincial preserves. Finally, as we had to expect sooner or later, the federal election in October 1972 brought a resounding denial of the theory according to which it was possible to install the 'power of Quebec' in Ottawa. And to get it out —

During the years 1970-2 we were in a situation where the anticipated hundreds of millions failed to materialize, while the federal hold tightened at the expense both of the Quebec government's current prerogatives and the prospects for those powers it had long been claiming. This hold actually grew with the increase of French-speaking Quebeckers in the federal Cabinet and Ottawa officialdom. Paradoxically, their presence lent new impetus to the normal centripetal tendency of the federal régime. On the one hand, momentarily conspicuous in the federal machine, these Quebeckers wanted to do something, and they were aware on the other of the social and economic problems of Quebec. Yet they saw little objection to the enlargement of a federal power that now seemed less 'dangerous' for Quebec because, as French-speaking Quebeckers, they influenced it. And they had to demonstrate Ottawa's concern for Quebec's people in a way that would check the rise of independentist feeling. They turned quite openly to the means offered by the administration in which they were working: direct intervention, conditional grants, new programs in grey zones, insistence on Ottawa's 'national' responsibilities, refusal to limit the central government's classic prerogatives, public policy statements on exclusively

Quebec problems, and so forth. In short, these Quebec representatives probably wanted to do the right thing, but for that they had to fall back on methods that would necessarily involve the weakening of the power of Quebec. Some of them worked consciously to weaken this power, the mere existence of which could, as they saw it, provide a base for Quebec independentism. This was a danger to ward off at all cost.

We must not hope therefore for anything but a modest return from a federal government strongly influenced by Quebeckers. The fault is not theirs. It is impossible to get more out of the present system than the system can give. Quebec may get as much money as it can from Ottawa by exploiting all existing federal programs to the maximum and marshalling all the administrative devices it can find, either alone or with assistance from federal politicians and officials whose home province is Quebec. This procedure can involve the fairly unpleasant necessity of appearing to beg for favours while giving in to specious schemes that promote federal tendencies to paternalistic condescension. Moreover we might also arrive, by a curious political spiral, at the stage of entrenchment of an ever more marked dependence on Ottawa; and we will have done so because there were Quebeckers in Ottawa honestly doing everything in their power to help Quebec as far as the present Ottawa-province power structure allowed.

The present structure: this is the major factor that is never given enough weight in attempts to evaluate Quebec's advantage in having Ottawa representatives in positions to win the central government's acceptance of Quebec political views. I am dealing here with a deep misunderstanding from which Quebec public men are the first to suffer, a misunderstanding that was veiled in 1970-1 by the superficial optimism surrounding the arrival of 'paying' federalism. The vast majority of Quebec federal ministers and MPs are strictly federal in their allegiance. They go to Ottawa to play a federal role and participate in the operation of the central régime. They get themselves elected as members of political groups that want not only to maintain the current federal system but also to make the government of Canada more effective, more ubiquitous — in short, a more powerful institution. This is perfectly natural, and it would be out of place, to say the least, if we criticized these people for their loyalty to the present political system. There are, of course, exceptional cases of Quebec federal MPs rising either from the fringes of the ruling party or from the opposition benches to defend Quebec positions or cast themselves as their spokesmen. Their marginality or quality as opposition members, if it does not tarnish their possible sincerity, much reduces the effectiveness of whatever support they can give Quebec.

When Quebec calls for a far-reaching reform of the whole political system in Canada, federal members from Quebec are probably the last people it should rely on to promote its views. As the achievement of these objectives would, by a reduction of Ottawa's hold over Quebec, entail substantial change in the role and prestige of these men, it would be perfectly unreasonable to expect them to commit political hara-kiri. When, for instance, we look at Quebec's constitutional stand on social policy, we immediately see that no federal representative from Quebec could support it. Paramountcy would mean these Ottawa parliamentarians would lose their chance to tell the voters about the generosity of their party or their government. The same applies in terms of all Quebec positions challenging the current federal spending power, whether in the form of bursaries for university research, grants to theatre companies, or to enterprises like Opportunities for Youth and Local Initiatives. In other words, any program produced by Ottawa, and which in the view of federal parliamentarians helps bring the federal government into more immediate contact with the citizen, falls into a category of federal activities whose transfer to Quebec is unimaginable for our people in Ottawa, whatever Quebec's reasons for wanting it may be. Under duress these members will agree that Quebec — without of course leaving out the other provinces — will be consulted in the elaboration of federal policy and even assigned an active role in carrying it through. This kind of thinking was present in the Quebec-Ottawa discussions on family allowances in the spring of 1972.

What federal members from Quebec dread above all else is entrapment in areas that generally arouse little voter interest: foreign affairs, the finances of central government, overseas investment, wheat exports, and so on. At a time when governments are playing an increasingly greater role in the citizen's daily life, this concern is shared by the whole central administration. The result is not only a deep reluctance to abandon certain areas of activity to Quebec, and in the event to other provinces as well, but also an intensifying desire to interfere in areas close to the people, areas frequently found outside federal jurisdiction and which become more and more interesting as our society evolves. These are also the areas most likely to attract the attention of citizens' groups and other organizations of that type. In a previous chapter, we read the announcement of the federal quest for this kind of close contact. Federal parliamentarians from Quebec may be prepared to give financial assistance to the administration of a province, but we certainly cannot ask them to participate in the building of a Quebec state. Incompatibility is total at this point, and it takes a strong dose of fantasy to persist in the belief that federal Quebec members can play the part of a sort of pro-Quebec fifth column in the central administration of Canada. The reasoning that holds for politicians holds too, *mutatis mutandis*, for federal civil service personnel. No official wants to see the range of his responsibilities reduced, as with that goes his prestige and often his salary. Officials certainly do not run the government, in Ottawa or in Quebec City, but it is obvious that they will be more than reluctant in the face of any suggestion that seems likely to curtail their ambitions. Rather they try, quite naturally, and often with great sincerity, to find technical objections to Quebec's aims, and even incline to embellish their significance. They make federal politicians the gift of a clear conscience by proving that Quebec's positions, even if in the last analysis they are not without foundation, raise almost insurmountable practical difficulties.

And if by chance it did happen that a federal minister nourished a little sympathy towards a particular political stand taken by Quebec, and yearned inwardly for its acceptance by Ottawa, the natural loyalty that tends to develop between the political men and the employees of the state would probably prompt his defence of the civil servants whose jobs might be affected by a transfer of responsibilities to Quebec City. If, exceptionally, this loyalty were absent, the minister would still have to convince his Cabinet colleagues and all the federal opponents he would undoubtedly meet along the way. We may presume these opponents would be numerous.

No doubt these are reasons why no federal Quebec minister during the past ten years has come out in agreement with Quebec's political stand on the division of powers, whatever premier expressed it. A fifth column that did not once, through a single federal representative, express itself on basic issues in the period when Quebec was pressing its positions with the greatest insistence is probably a fifth column that does not exist. In fact the real fifth column is to be found in Quebec City itself. It has not been placed there by the central government, but is no less objectively in Ottawa's service when the occasion arises. Its members are primarily a few ministers, Members of the National Assembly, and high officials easily impressed by the personnel and methods of the central government. For them, federal decisions and policies are born with a stigma of infallibility. Among them, one notes individuals quickened by an ineradicable inferiority complex. Included also are a few people looking forward to an eventual federal career, or anxious to cultivate a 'good image' with certain federal people with whom their functions occasionally put them in contact. Here too are some whose Ottawa ties in politics or friendship remain very close.

This 'sixth column' in Quebec City is not heavily staffed, however. Its influence is extremely variable and rather fleeting. I refer to it here because its activity is particularly marked when the government in power is anxious, for tactical or other reasons, to sidestep federal-provincial confrontations and maintain the closest possible relations with Ottawa. 'Unconditional federalists' in the political and administrative Quebec ranks see this as a hopeful occasion to shine. Ottawa will sometimes manage to use them without their knowledge to sow division in Quebec and produce concessions or information that would never be delivered by those ministers and officials more faithful to a genuine Quebec perspective.

It also happens that certain politicians and administrators in Quebec City are so opposed to potential independence that they see federal intervention as separatism insurance. Without openly working for this intervention they are not always dissatisfied to note an increasing federal grip. When federal-provincial conflicts arise, their autonomist inclinations are not especially pronounced. In their quest for what they see as 'harmony' between the capitals they can inadvertently give the central régime the means of further penetration into provincial preserves. So it is that up against Ottawa, and in times when need is urgent for cohesion in all its forces, the Quebec government sometimes sabotages itself.

14
The Silent Majority

Neither side in Quebec-Ottawa conflict is shy about citing public opinion, which they invariably suppose to be solid behind them. The situation is bizarre: the same population in Quebec is portrayed as backing contradictory stands at the same time. Instances are many. For years, Maurice Duplessis rejected the federal government's claim to finance the universities directly, since in his opinion Quebeckers were unalterably opposed to federal intervention in that realm. At the same moment, however, there were Quebec professors calling for federal funds and attacking the Duplessis stand. In 1964 Quebec won the day on tax sharing, pensions, and the contracting out of shared cost programs. The government referred repeatedly to the presumed support of Quebec's people for its approach in the tough negotiations with Ottawa. When, a few years later, Ottawa launched a recovery program for the ground lost in 1964, Canadians, including Quebeckers, were assumed to be in agreement with the central government's aims. And as Quebec City moved to block the federal desire for reconquest, appeal was made to Quebec public opinion. Dozens of similar examples could be cited. The question is, how can Ottawa and Quebec simultaneously, and often on opposing views, refer to Quebec public opinion as a basis for their claims? One thought that may occur is that it comes about because the general population has no interest in these repeated confrontations, and the use of its 'opinion' as a weapon by one government or the other is simply a gesture referrable to the kind of political process we have. Obviously, in intergovernmental dealings, the population's presumed wishes are easily touted without any effort having been made to ascertain their nature or intensity. We might say that these illusions tend to be ritual truisms adding nothing to the cogency of the arguments advanced, but their absence would be likely to reinforce the adversary or make Quebec-Ottawa conflict look like nothing more than a politicians' pecking-order squabble. And yet we would be wrong in believing that, in a general sense, the population lacks interest in these subjects. Of course, they are not thought of unremittingly, and many other concerns claim the public's attention. People may also tire of the debates, especially if they are long and technical. In fact, here as in a number of other areas, citizens have a tendency to remember only the most salient features of the events and carry away nothing but general, sometimes mistaken impressions. This does not mean that their attitude is one of indifference, however.

The reader may already have noted that it is the unconditional federalists who raise the greatest fuss about the Quebec population's supposed indifference to federal-provincial issues. The reaction is a defensive one. Federalists like to think that the opponents of the present system, whether independentists or merely reformers, have no public behind them. As such issues as unemployment, inadequate wages, or illness, are clearly day-to-day concerns for those citizens suffering from them and the even greater number worrying about them, these federalists decide that the 'constitutional' issues must take a decidedly secondary place in the 'minds of the people.' They forget that the population may be interested in several issues at the same time, that anxiety about unemployment does not rule out consideration of Quebec's future and its problems within the present federal system. Those wanting to 'prove' lack of Quebec concern with these questions sometimes cite the fact that they come near the bottom of the lists in the public opinion polls. But we would have to know how the questions are asked, something the reports do not always reveal. Moreover, reports on surveys of a very general nature on public aspirations often include only those subjects achieving a certain percentage, while other and much more numerous topics fail to make the published list. The 'constitutional problems' are always there.

Indeed, the federalist terminology is symptomatic in itself. There is talk of 'constitutional' problems, but none of the role and future of Quebec. The word 'constitutional' has a juridical connotation, reminding us of high-flown texts of law, hard to fathom even if one has the time to look them over. It must be admitted that if the Quebec problem is reduced to such dry and unventilated terms it will obviously attract only a handful of specialists. It would be a little like discussing health in strictly biochemical terms. Yet this Quebec problem has a significance that extends far beyond the merely juridical. It is highly political as well, since it has to do with the division of powers between Ottawa and Quebec, and hence with the nature and attributions of the governments concerned. Very few people are untouched by this, as its evidence is manifold and concrete, even if it sometimes appears to lack 'constitutional' ramifications so far as the average citizen is concerned. Lack of consistency in certain social measures affects citizens who may not always be aware that the problem is the consequence of concurrent Quebec and Ottawa operation in the income security field. The unemployed working man may be in that condition because of a federal anti-inflationary move fairly inconspicuous in Quebec but worrisome in Ontario or British Columbia. The family in an underprivileged region may observe that nothing or virtually nothing is being done to improve their lot, but are likely unaware that governmental inaction can sometimes be laid at the door of Quebec-Ottawa confrontation. I could continue citing examples of this kind, although the aim here is not to assign the guilt for all the average citizen's inconvenience to today's federal system. The point to remember is that the system's operation in current circumstances can have side-effects on individuals without those individuals always being conscious of them.

This seemingly coincidental support Quebeckers give to contradictory Quebec and Ottawa positions may also, some think, be explained by the fact that the average citizen does not particularly worry about which government ought to be functioning in a given instance, provided one of them does something. Often advanced by unconditional federalists, this argument is not without an element of truth. In many cases, citizens are not altogether aware of which government holds authority over what. Especially if there is urgency in the case, an understandable exasperation or impatience may temporarily push aside potentially decisive considerations; when fire threatens, we do not care whether the firemen come from our own municipality or outside it. Behaviour under pressure, however, dictated by the gravity of a situation or else quite simply by a perfectly understandable ignorance of constitutional subtlety, still should not let us think that Quebeckers are generally and regularly indifferent to the identity of the government from which they expect solutions for their difficulties or a fresh orientation for their society. In their view, the main government has been and still is the one in Quebec City. The federal authorities have grasped this sufficiently to embark on a program, accentuated in the past few years, of forging new links with the citizen of Quebec.

How, finally, do we explain the situation? The inconsistency seems very real. Political history, however, inclines me to the view that Quebeckers are a consistent people. The 'inconsistency' more often noted by observers is undoubtedly the election of opposing political parties to Ottawa and Quebec City. Looking at this a bit more closely, though without going into a lengthy analysis of electoral motivation, I seem to see a kind of logic in Quebec's popular choices. My theory is that Quebeckers quite simply have been defending their own interests. They have been less concerned to send a government to Quebec City to oppose the one in Ottawa than to vote for the federal or provincial party that looked likely at any given moment to give them the greatest individual or collective advantage. They were looking for the individual benefits on the

Quebec side, since they saw that government as having a day-to-day presence and effect. Collective benefits, those embracing the French-speaking society of Quebec as a whole, figured less in provincial elections. Whatever party was in power, Quebec's government was naturally bound to concern itself with them. Quebeckers have traditionally expected less in the way of personal benefit from federal governments, but have still hoped they would advance the French-Canadian cause in relation to English Canada. They have generally voted Liberal because the Conservatives and then the Progressive Conservatives impressed them as less favourable to the French Canadians. Quebeckers delivered their most massive tory verdict in 1958, a time when they were convinced the party was heading for power in Ottawa and that their best course was to contribute to its election. In 1968 and 1972, a large proportion of them voted for Pierre Elliott Trudeau because in their eyes he was a French Canadian like themselves. The same reflex had come into play when Louis St Laurent and, in the last century, Wilfrid Laurier, were candidates for party leadership.

In short, the Quebec federal vote has always been a nationalist vote, even when it benefited Trudeau, a dedicated adversary of Quebec nationalism although not then perceived as such by the Quebec voters. They saw him rather as an eminently representative French Canadian resolved to take up the active defence of French Canada, a notion pressed on Quebec again in the 1972 contest by the Liberal machine. Quebeckers' behaviour at the polls is thus more or less consistent in terms of benefits expected, as is very likely the case in other democracies. Given the present system, they opt instinctively for governments in Ottawa as well as Quebec City that seem the likeliest to generate individual and collective advantages for them, and they are not, as some like to think, trying to 'divide and rule' by choosing opposing parties on a basis of elaborate electoral calculations. As far as Ottawa is concerned, at all events, they are not the only ones doing the choosing; they are simply aiming to get the most out of each government.

Quebeckers may be consistent, but my contradiction remains unexplained. In tackling it I should first make allowance for possible lack of information. I have already noted that Quebeckers, like citizens everywhere, remember government positions only in their most general aspects. Sometimes only the specialists and addicts of Quebec-Ottawa affairs can indicate the technical areas in which the two profoundly differ. Let us take the case of constitutional paramountcy in family allowances. For the Quebec government, this means that with concurrent legislation the provincial law must prevail. In the fall of 1971 and the spring of 1972, however, the central government advanced the counterclaim that no constitutional change was needed for Quebec to determine administratively the rates of payment to be made, providing only that they were consistent with certain federal standards. Some who were anxious to avoid another conflict chose to see in this line of reasoning a species of paramountcy which, though not strictly in line with Quebec's initial claim, still fell in with its concrete objectives. In fact we were not talking about the same thing at all, for the federal proposal rejected Quebec's constitutional claims. In addition, sensing that there was no victory to be had in this area, Quebec let it be understood for months on end that basic agreement had been reached, and only a few questions of detail remained to be resolved. It was not until a press conference in May 1972 that Quebec's social affairs minister took it on himself to shed a little light on the situation, and admitted that the administrative arrangements Ottawa proposed would not give Quebec the paramountcy it was looking for. We may assume that the general public had meanwhile lost interest in the issue, lost as it was amid such subtle distinctions. How could the public take sides when it had been told that the two were in agreement, or close to it?

In order to amass apparent support, Ottawa makes regular use of ambiguities, together with the frequent impossibility of the public's sorting things out in highly technical federal-provincial discussion. Ottawa can thus easily advertise its desire to decentralize administration and make a fine impression on a Quebec public that will not suspect that the decentralization will apply only to areas of current administration, and do nothing to put a stop to the gradual gathering of important governmental prerogatives in Ottawa's hands. When, in May 1972, the Quebec prime minister announced his intention of challenging the unlimited federal spending power, a challenge already issued by his predecessors, the prime minister of Canada argued that the question was not so simple as he made it appear, for it was this same spending power that made it possible for the central authority to pay Quebec more than half a billion dollars in equalization. Again, they were not talking about the same thing. The prime minister of Quebec was not challenging the system of equalization, and was perfectly aware that it flowed from the federal spending power. He was aiming instead at a reduction of federal freedom of intervention in areas of provincial authority. The Canadian prime minister drew popular attention to an aspect of the spending power that is currently beneficial to the people of Quebec, without lingering over the problems raised by massive federal intervention in sectors outside Ottawa's jurisdiction. It is not hard to understand public confusion when disputes are presented in this way, and that leads me to a factor other than simple lack of information. In addition to everything else, federal and Quebec statements always contain undeniable elements of truth, even if their ultimate objectives are contradictory. Quebeckers may feel in agreement with a particular argument, no matter who advances it. The public must form its opinion not on the basis of a problem but on accidental or secondary aspects as strategically displayed.

Quebec has long been asking for more adequate distribution of the country's fiscal and financial resources. The people of Quebec are not unaware of their government's large financial needs, and thus support the demands. There was a partial net transfer in 1965 and an improvement of equalization in 1966. Ottawa's finance minister told the Tax Structure Committee meeting in the latter year that the federal authorities had gone as far as they could go in that direction, and it would now be up to provinces to levy taxes for their own administration. According to the minister, Ottawa would be needing all its revenue to discharge its functions and respond to citizens' demands. Neither the Quebec population nor that of any other province in the country could begin by disagreeing in principle with such a stand, seeming as it did to proceed from the purest common sense. People were not aware, however, of Ottawa's determination to keep all its resources for various new initiatives, most of them affecting areas which were provincial according to Quebec — health insurance, community development, culture — or else to consolidate or enhance the federal role in sectors already under Quebec fire. They were playing on an old ambiguity: the tasks Ottawa wanted to take on were not necessarily federal (according to Quebec) but could easily be justified in terms of precedents, or declared as involving the 'national interest.' This whole aspect of Ottawa's 1966 stand went uncommented upon by the federal government. It was hard for Quebec to highlight Ottawa's aims since, despite its moral conviction, it lacked irrefutable proof. It took the following years to show us the full scope of the freedom the central government kept for itself in 1966, but the realization came too late. In any event, using another of its advance techniques, Ottawa was always careful to put forward programs responding to specific needs in the population, which effectively stopped provincial governments from voicing strong objection. Blocking Quebec action, Quebec City would often find itself in the unenviable position of depriving citizens of money the federal authorities were all set to spend. Proclamation of autonomist views in such circumstances calls for a large measure of courage.

Some members of government in Quebec look back to crises such as those over conscription which raised Quebeckers in near unanimity against Ottawa. Passively, they hope history will be good enough to repeat itself, producing unequivocal popular support and helping them against the subtle infiltration of the federal government. They are forgetting, however, that at the time of conscription and other such crises the issues were clear. Quebeckers knew where to find their trenches. This is no longer the case, at least while the usages and customs of present-day Canadian federalism exist, and while Ottawa can nourish that very convenient ambiguity.

But is the Quebec government likely to be in a position to dispel the ambiguity itself, and go after the massive public support it pines for? At times, yes, but generally the reply must be no, if that Quebec government is committed to the defence of the present federal system. To get the support, it would have to place the blame squarely on the acquired federal prerogatives that underpin the system, not to mention engage in a wearisome guerrilla campaign that would lead logically to a blanket challenge of the system. The people of Quebec thus find themselves in a situation where the normal working of the political system and the strategies of the governments involved produce confusion, and may occasionally give rise to the impression among those inclined to think that way that the population is less anxious than formerly to safeguard what we used to call provincial 'autonomy.' Any Quebec approval of federal policies, even won precariously in the circumstances described above, even if only apparent and evidenced simply by a sort of neutrality, gives Ottawa justification for its plans, and 'proof' for other provinces that Quebeckers have really changed. In this way the people of Quebec can be used to further a subtle centralization whose political consequences will have been carefully concealed from them.

Should we conclude that Quebeckers have determined their duty as opposition to all federal initiatives, and that consequently their acceptance of any Ottawa policy is a sort of historical contradiction or even treason against their natural aspirations? Not at all, and this is worth emphasizing. What is serious here is not the fact that Quebeckers, like citizens of any province, may sometimes favour policies proposed by the central government. After all, Ottawa well knows how, in the realms of its proper jurisdiction, to put together valid projects.

What is serious is the trend. Pestered by two governments looking for support, each controlling areas intimately affecting them, Quebeckers have been moved by force of circumstance not to reduce their natural allegiance to the government of Quebec, but to pay more attention than formerly to what Ottawa might do in those vital areas where it has gained a foothold. As it is fairly infrequent for them to be called upon for a judgement on the cogency of the federal presence in these areas, and as at all events Ottawa is careful to keep the issue out of debate — something noted in the four years of the constitutional review — Quebeckers and even their government are obliged to set this federal fact aside and be satisfied with expressing opinions on the details of Ottawa's planning. This leaves Ottawa in an excellent position to interpret Quebec thinking about the technical aspects of current federal programs as implicit approval of its presence in these areas, and acceptance of its 'national' role.

If Quebeckers are bedevilled as regards federal-provincial relations, they are in equal trouble among themselves with the numerous political factions seeking their support. First come the federal and provincial parties: we have already seen how a federal parliamentarian from Quebec is unable to give support to the growth of Quebec power. Nevertheless, he has been chosen by the same voters who choose members for the National Assembly, and the latter, though not all in favour of an increase in the power of Quebec, are at least generally opposed to its being cut down. Pinned between two governments, Quebeckers are also pinned between two groups of political parties, each following its own philosophy.

And this is not all. Quebec parties themselves, either for ideological reasons or for motives of immediate electoral advantage, sometimes confound the confusion by modelling their own positions on those of the federal government. Quebec's international adventures produced an obvious instance of this political oscillation. In the days of the Quiet Revolution, the Union nationale saw all extraterritorial interest on the part of the ruling Liberals as simply an excrescence of the policy of aggrandizement they generally disapproved of. In office after 1966, the Union nationale changed its mind, and its reign saw diversification and enlargement of Quebec's international relations. Meanwhile the Liberals were passing up almost no opportunity to criticize this development on the grounds that there were more pressing needs to be attended to. Back in office, although as an assurance of good understanding with their Ottawa confrères they pretended to rein in these external activities, the same Liberal party was no less official in its assertions of their necessity. Now in opposition, the Union nationale kept a close watch in the hope of catching the government out, as it had during the Quiet Revolution years before. This party-political behaviour could be shown through many other examples. Liberal and Union nationale members — and now the Ralliement Créditiste, though in different terms as they have never held office — will take turns blaming one another either for giving way to Ottawa or for not working closely enough with the central government. It is more and more unusual for the National Assembly to express unanimity in the field of Quebec-Ottawa relations. Before 1966, such occasions were more frequent.

Apart from their source in party-political rivalry, these recent developments owe much to the increased acuteness of the Quebec-Ottawa problem and the polarization in opinions. Supporters, conscious or unconscious, of federalism or independence, now have more and more frequent opportunities to pronounce, not on vast and vaguely worded general objectives, but on a number of very practical issues with many factors to be considered — technical, economic, or social, in addition to political. The ambiguity noted in Quebec-Ottawa conflict is also at work in Quebec itself, among these parties and within them. A Quebec political party is thus perfectly able to turn down a government proposal on technical grounds without having to pronounce on its federal-provincial aspect. If the proposal is 'nationalist' in type, its rejection by Quebeckers in the

National Assembly will be grist to a federal mill that creaks for want of it, even if the reasons for rejection have nothing at all to do with Quebec-Ottawa conflict.

Among the vehicles of expression and influence of public opinion — the papers, radio, and television — as well as in the various social or economic associations, we find the same mixture of ambiguity, party-political allegiance, and incomplete information. The effects are similar. The practical result of all this is that, though most Quebeckers do remain basically and strongly convinced that the Quebec government should have real power and not leave the responsibility to Ottawa, it is not easy for them, in the normal course of events, to make this conviction felt. In fact, as we have just seen, the present division of powers between Ottawa and Quebec, the current federal-provincial pattern, and the presence of rival federal and provincial parties confuse the citizenry and produce a jamming effect that works against the identification, essential as it often is in political debate, of the principal and accessory, the permanent and provisional, the fundamental and secondary. To this some reply, and with reason, that the situation is inherent in the federal system. We are indulging in utopian wishful thinking if we wait for Quebec public opinion, in a sort of sudden awakening, to mass itself one day behind the Quebec government and give that institution the unequivocal support it wants in the fight against centralization. The truth is that the system divides Quebeckers against themselves.

15

The Magnetic Pendulum:
Growing Imbalance

We have seen Quebec as deprived of effective and powerful arms, in a sense victimized by adverse forces emanating from a system that divides it against itself and sets at odds the sources of support on which it would at first seem natural for it to rely. Yet can Quebec still not see these simply as passing difficulties, while placing its trust in that deep-seated tendency to balance which, in the opinion of some, has characterized Canadian federalism from the outset?

In all its varieties, federalism assumes the existence of two orders of government, federal and provincial or, if one prefers, national and regional. It also assumes some sort of division between the two of legislative prerogative as well as fiscal and financial resources. A federal system is a dynamic political organization, producing sets of circumstances which in turn influence the functioning of the system. To reflect this reality, we often have to recognize the impossibility of placing the two levels of government in watertight compartments, so that the federal order would not penetrate areas reserved to provinces, and vice versa. This impossibility of hermetically sealed power sectors is clearly a consequence of the fact that areas of governmental action are contiguous, and anything done in one produces reactions in another. It is also a consequence, however, of the general impracticability of constantly changing the prerogatives assigned to a particular order of government. By the effects of centripetal or centrifugal forces which themselves depend on economic, technological, or cultural elements in our situations, a federal or provincial administration may acquire new powers while it functions, powers not mentioned or provided for explicitly in the initial lists entrusted to one or the other. In other words, a constitution is not amended annually, and as a result, since the realm of governmental activity keeps enlarging nonetheless, new sectors of public intervention are taken over by either 'national' or 'regional' authorities as circumstances allow. These circumstances can confer advantage on one governmental order or the other to change profoundly the operation of the entire system. If we are to deliver a verdict on the Canadian federal system, therefore, we must reach our verdict less on the basis of theoretical guiding principles or purely constitutional thinking than in the light of the system's tangible results. Some will claim a federal system cannot tend to centralization since, by definition, federalism presupposes balance between governments. This claim is as valid as the one that social disparity is unknown in a socialist system because socialism exists specifically to end disparities.

In itself, a federal system of government is neither better nor worse than any other. It is generally better suited to countries with large areas and varied populations, but it does occur too in small countries such as Switzerland. It may be thought admirable or detestable depending on our criteria, themselves dictated by the political objectives we adopt. If, more than anything else, we are looking for administrative decentralization, a federal system is probably better than a unitary one. If we are aiming to make it possible for diverse nationalities to safeguard some of their peculiar cultural traits, again a federal system can have advantages to offer. On the other side of the coin, efficiency and dispatch in public administration are better realized in a government of the unitary type, which does not have to be concerned to organize its policies in conjunction with those of regional governments or take their potential opposition into account.

What are the criteria to be used for the Canadian system? There are many possibilities. We must certainly start by rejecting any that depend on secondary elements, or any that are hard to attribute directly to the federal structure. It would be ridiculous to boast of federalism's merits in terms of the redistribution of wealth to which it would lead, or the development of the Canadian Arctic that the system would be supposed to facilitate. The same type of remark applies when federalism's champions stress the strength the system gives a big country such as Canada: in a unitary state the strength would still exist, and might even be greater. Somewhat more weighty are pro-federalist arguments relating to the potential for development and expansion the system offers the various cultural groups living in the country. It may be that federalism is better suited to populations made up of a number of ethnic groups. Be it said in passing, however, that the French-Canadian community is not merely one of Canada's ethnic minorities.

I will not review all arguments for or against Canadian federalism in this chapter, but limit myself to what seems essential within the parameters set for this book, and make my judgement of the system in terms of its effect on the behaviour and attributions of the government of Quebec, hence on the only political power Quebeckers have permanently and directly at their command. The system will earn my acceptance, therefore, to the extent that it lets Quebec power function as a true government. By the same token it will be less acceptable to the extent that it tends to erode the powers of the government of Quebec and relegate it to the status of a mere regional administration, bereft of meaningful prerogative. In this chapter and the next, the facts will lead to the conclusion that present-day Canadian federalism tends inevitably to debase Quebec's power.

There are some who refuse to judge federalism on the basis of its influence on the powers of the various governments. For them, these powers are of little importance, and what counts is the standard of economic and cultural life afforded the population. It is absolutely certain that the standard of living, or still better, the quality of life, is of capital importance, and it is for precisely this reason that we ought to be asking ourselves what would happen to the quality of Quebec life in the middle and long terms if Quebeckers did not have control of powerful political machinery. From this standpoint, the existence and action of an authentic Quebec government are prior conditions for the quality of life.

Other theories that are not yet fashionable, but which may well become so, hold it wrong and anachronistic to judge federalism on the basis of the notion of 'power.' Rather, federalism is supposed to be a way of thinking, a permanent quest for compromise, a deep desire for balance, a persuasive will to live together despite cultural differences, and so on. All this is fine, even admirable. Political sainthood and governmental abnegation, in short the federalism of the angels, are doubtless highly to be prized. In the real world, however, it happens that the governments in a federation act, if they are orderly, in terms of the powers they possess, and if they are dynamic, in terms of those they regard as necessary. In these circumstances, since for better or for worse power is the source and measure of action, we must steel ourselves to the evaluation of powers. It is the levy demanded of us, in this business of federalism, for dealing in concrete terms.

Many are the historians and jurists who believed they saw a succession of eras of centralization and decentralization in Canada. What they thought they saw is the notorious 'pendulum effect.' For a time, Ottawa manages to play a decisive and predominant role in Canadian affairs as a whole, and then for a time it is the turn of the provinces, hence a movement of decentralization. And so it goes. This 'pendulum effect' comes in very handy for certain defenders of the status quo, and makes them the gift of a good conscience. If we are to believe them, Quebeckers have no need to be all that concerned about what might happen to their government, since centralization, when it occurs, never lasts indefinitely; sooner or later, the provinces will be on top once more.

This point of view arises from confusion as to the nature of this decentralization. Once it is dispelled we see that, contrary to general opinion, the 'pendulum effect' has never obtained in Canada, at least in those terms in which it is usually understood. Over more than a century, we have seen a deep-rooted process that tends increasingly to centralization of the true levers of political power. The fact that this process has not always followed a regular rhythm, and has occasionally given rise to provincial reaction, fosters the belief in a sort of constant power-shuttle between Ottawa and the provinces. It is nothing of the sort. When the pendulum seems to be heading back in the direction of the provinces, it is much more because circumstances have allowed them to produce more initiative and innovation in their own areas, while at the same time the federal role is less brilliant, than because they helped themselves to federal preserves. During the half century after Confederation, the provinces, especially Ontario and Quebec, made special efforts to get confirmation of the powers they believed to be theirs under the constitution, but which were challenged by the centripetal Ottawa mentality. The reaction was basically defensive, and not a drive for conquest. It bore fruit, but it would be an exaggeration to conclude that it caused Ottawa to vacate important fields of its jurisdiction.

To get a clearer idea of how things really are let us take a contemporary example. Everyone is convinced a priori that the 'Quiet Revolution' coincided with, or gave rise to, a period of intense decentralization, described as unprecedented. Beginning with Premier Jean Lesage, it is generally regarded as ending when the Trudeau government reached Ottawa. In terms of the pendulum effect we would thus expect to see a reasonably impressive roster of provincial conquest and reconquest. In fact there was nothing of the kind. Except for fiscal arrangements, adjusted slightly in the provinces' favour, only Quebec seems to have made any real advance. But, as I have noted, there was less an advance than a partial and temporary suspension, from 1964 to around 1968, of a movement of centralization. What gains there were did not come with any seal of permanence. Unless we take it that in order to validate this pendulum effect in federalist eyes provinces need merely hold centralization off for a few years, we have to conclude that the famous power-shuttle is a deception.

It might be said that although this supposed pendulum was not seen to best effect in the Quiet Revolution, it was more active during earlier periods of decentralization. Without going into a complete study of the development of federal and provincial powers over the past century, I will simply note that never in the entire hundred years has there been a conclusive Ottawa retreat, even if federal plans have sometimes had to be deferred for a while. Certainly, the central government has periodically tried to turn administrative tasks over to provinces, or return to them some it has assumed. Ottawa has let its power of disallowance of provincial law fall into disuse, although it made free use of it in the period immediately after the BNA Act. Ottawa has also refused on several occasions to increase its involvement in the running of a given area of activity provinces wanted to relinquish. And certain preliminary federal proposals in constitutional review tended either to confirm to provinces powers not clearly allocated to them before, or else somewhat limit certain habitual Ottawa prerogatives such as the spending power. Again, time after time there was question of federal-provincial administrative arrangements under which provinces could enjoy greater freedom in the conception and implementation of federal laws such as family allowances. Many convinced federalists use these displays of seeming decentralist desire to prove that the division of powers is far from unalterable, and the Canadian political system capable of adapting to circumstance and legitimate provincial demands. They use them too as evidence of the federal-provincial pendulum. We must realize, however, that Ottawa has never, at any time since Confederation, handed over a single prerogative. Nor, despite some protest from provinces, has there been any hesitation on Ottawa's part in getting involved in areas it sees as decisive. Beyond the political vicissitudes and federal-provincial disputes that sometimes incline us to credit the pendulum's existence, Ottawa has never lost sight of the essential, and it has always had, if not the conscious art, at least the instinctive reaction of consolidating its position in truly decisive sectors. It is worth noting that the importance of a sector may vary with the times: Ottawa held the establishment of a health insurance scheme as an essential social innovation that had to be directly guided by the federal authorities, but now that medicare is entrenched, operations may be handed over to the provinces with appropriate financial compensation and the proviso that systems be maintained and comparable with each other.

What holds for the past will hold for the future, assuming the present political system continues. Though we have seen an acute centralizing spasm in the past few years, it is quite possible that passing inclinations to the contrary may appear in years to come, and if that were the case, attempts would be made to clothe them in a spectacular quality. Except with an overall change of system, however, this decentralization will doubtless affect only those administrative functions Ottawa sees as dispensable without danger to its general preponderance. It is by no means impossible that we will again live through a period of decentralization such as that sparked by Quebec's Quiet Revolution. At the same time, we are now better aware of the limits and fleeting character of such an operation.

Any analysis of alleged power exchanges between orders of government in Canada has to consider the administrative arrangements involving them. These may sometimes be far from insignificant. To the degree that they are rare or numerous, such arrangements may give the impression of centralizing or decentralizing processes. In fact, however, they have very little to do with any real transfer of power. We may imagine an extreme case in which all legislative power is Ottawa's, and the provinces have all the execution. There is no chance of this case coming to pass, but if it should, the provinces would clearly appear to hold enormous power attributions. Yet we must remind ourselves at this point that they would have them only to the degree that Ottawa handed them over. This really means that the source and control of power, even in my fantastic theory, would be situated in Ottawa, which would then have a total right of confirmation over all provincial activity and could challenge any arrangement agreed to beforehand. In the terms of my extreme case this kind of arrangement, which may be called ad hoc, could in no sense stand as a valid substitute for clearly defined legislative powers. They have no guarantee of permanence, and moreover, presuppose that provinces agree to uphold standards made by the sovereign authority of Ottawa. In their own way, federal-provincial fiscal arrangements also fall into this ad hoc category. Frequently advanced as proof of the decentralization of the system is the fact that in 1964 the province won appreciable fiscal abatements, and Ottawa lost a portion of its fiscal resources. Certainly these abatements, combined with their predecessors, will give provinces more financial freedom to deal with their already recognized prerogatives, but we must stress that they in no way affect the federal taxing power, as great today as it was before the abatements while that of the provinces is no greater than it was ten or twenty years ago. And it is this taxing power that let Ottawa move into the whole fiscal field during the Second World War.

Analyzing Canada's development since Confederation, and taking as my criteria these ad hoc arrangements together with temporary adjustments dictated by circumstance, I will in fact discover a federal-provincial pendulum of sorts. I would also encounter it if I measured the relative intensity of federal and provincial activity from one period to another, or the repercussions of federal or provincial influence in public life. None of this assumes any actual transfer of powers from one government to the other. It is when we imply that such transfers have constantly taken place, and by this token will continue to take place, that our interpretation falls into error.

In terms of the centralizing tendency I have indicated, federal powers have increased since the Canadian federation was formed. Some will be inclined to doubt this, replying rather that the increase has been on the provincial side. Let me stress at the outset that it is dangerous to compare the powers of a nineteenth-century or even an early twentieth-century state with those of the contemporary variety. The latter are more numerous, more varied, and above all more decisive as regards the life of their societies. Thus, qualitative and quantitative differences are important. For example, the Privy Council's recognition in 1883, against Ottawa opinion, of the constitutionality of provincial temperance laws, was undoubtedly important for that period, but it cannot compare with Ottawa's direct entry into urban affairs in 1970-1. In the first case, affirmation was accorded a provincial prerogative doubted by Ottawa, while in the second the federal government confirmed itself in a power of immense and daily consequence. The result is that even if the provinces had been completely successful over a period of fifty or sixty years in keeping intact the powers given them by the 1867 constitution, the federal advance of recent years would emerge as incomparably more decisive than all the provincial autonomy 'victories' lumped together.

It will also be objected that the federal powers have not grown as much as I am making out, since provincial budgets have risen more rapidly than Ottawa's, particularly during the decade past. In 1970, federal expenditure amounted to 40 per cent and provincial-municipal expenditure to 60 per cent of the total Canadian figure, as contrasted with percentages of 37 and 63 in 1952. The rate of increase in provincial expenditure has certainly been higher in this period, but this in no sense implies that provincial responsibilities are more significant than Ottawa's. If governmental powers do differ from one century to another, as I have noted, the same is true of federal and provincial powers. What we have to understand is that Ottawa is not trying indiscriminately to seize the greatest possible number of powers. It is endeavouring to secure control over those means liable to be of value in action and intervention, and they are not always the most expensive. Ottawa is also trying to exercise a right of confirmation over the control of certain important powers by provinces, for instance in working out 'national' standards. Provincial construction and maintenance of highways might well represent a much greater expenditure than certain federal activities such as scientific research or social development which have a greater overall impact on the society. Moreover, public disbursement in areas where provinces are already entrenched — education, health and welfare, and so on — has risen enormously in the past few years as these services were being extended and the salaries of those working in them increased. These extra costs have not meant any new power for the provinces as related to Ottawa's. On the contrary, they have provided justification for more generous and often more 'conditional' financial participation from the Ottawa side. The central government was absent from the fields of health, education, and social welfare when state expenditure was modest; at that time, most of the institutions involved relied on private initiative, with the province in a strictly auxiliary role. Then the provinces' governmental functions increased in consequence of industrialization and urban growth, and at the same time their new scope occurred in areas that were gradually passing from the private to the public sector, a process which in no way encroached on the federal attributions. In short, nothing more happened than a transfer of functions from the provincial private sector to the provincial public sector.

The pendulum theory just examined presupposes the existence somewhere in Canadian federalism of a sort of inherent balancing force, by virtue of which neither Ottawa nor the provinces may become too strong in relation to one another. This supposed equilibrium carries with it a corollary of 'free competition' between governments, a competition beneficial to the citizen. If one government, the province for example, were displaying inadequate creativity or even flagrant want of intelligence in essential policies, something that often occurs, a citizen could always depend on the arrival of his other government, in this case the federal. Federalism would thus lead to a useful balance between administrations, each considered as auxiliary to the other. If Quebec does not act, Ottawa can move in its place: so the argument goes. Its supporters cite a number of cases in which this is supposed to have happened. During the Duplessis régime, for instance, universities were short of funds, and Ottawa set up a grant program for them. In general, provinces have shown little initiative in terms of social security, but enlightened federal action has let citizens benefit nevertheless from aid programs of which they would otherwise have been deprived. In the past, basic rights might occasionally have been jostled, but happily, federal institutions such as the Supreme Court have been there to move effectively for the restoration of democratic freedoms in Quebec. And so forth: it is an attitude that can also be prompted by the more or less conscious feeling that one is 'better protected' by institutions strongly controlled by an English majority than by those of Quebec.

It would be possible to prove that the federal system itself is responsible for some of the unevenness from which Quebec politics over the years have not been entirely free. The inadequate division of resources between Ottawa and the provinces certainly shared responsibility with Duplessis himself for the plight of Quebec's universities. This inadequate distribution also largely explains why provinces have not shown more inventiveness in social legislation. Moreover, we too easily forget that provinces have often been innovative in that area, although Ottawa, with its resources and spending power, was afterwards able to move in on a grander scale. Regarding Duplessis' attitude to certain basic rights, I must point out that it was likely quite widespread in a population which had not then managed to move ahead as it would with the coming of the Quiet Revolution.

Those who summon the argument of healthy Ottawa-Quebec rivalry to the defence of the system are in fact sinning against federalism itself. They argue as if areas of jurisdiction belonged to any government, and when one fails the other has only to act. According to this line of reasoning, Quebec inactivity in education could bring Ottawa to the scene, or if measures for national defence seemed dubious to Quebec it could proceed to raise its own army. Federalists never push their argument that far, of course, and would never attempt to justify such flagrant assaults on the law of the land as the two just cited. They themselves recognize that the Quebec-Ottawa compensation pattern must not result in unconstitutionality.

Then what does their thinking mean? It means giving the central government a sort of active supervisory role over Quebec policies, which leads them in practice to assign Ottawa a corrective prerogative over Quebec 'errors' and thus deny Quebec's sovereignty within the limits of its constitutional power. They support everything in the present system that makes it possible to centralize decision making in Ottawa: spending power, grey areas of the constitution, more abundant resources than the provinces have, acceptance by the other provinces of Ottawa's 'national' role, and so on. The supposed fine balance of forces depicted in their interpretation of federalism encourages even stronger centralizing tendencies than those we would naturally expect.

This is not all. Defenders of Ottawa's corrective role are also sinning against democracy. Judgement on the facts and acts of their provincial government must come from the citizens and not from Ottawa. If it is permissible for the federal government to place its stamp on provincial situations that do not suit it — indirectly, for it cannot openly violate the constitution, say the advocates of 'corrective federalism' — what order of government is then to be responsible for the things that displease the citizens? How are they to express an opinion at election time? How, during a provincial election, can they vote against a federal government whose corrective action has not been appreciated? How, in a federal election, are they to pronounce against a provincial administration? The arguments for 'corrective federalism' leave us with this sort of unanswerable question.

Clearly, the federal-provincial pendulum is swinging towards Ottawa. Apart from purely juridical considerations, the experience of the past hundred years illuminates the flow of basic forces and long-term tendencies in the Canadian system which an examination limited to a period of a few years does not reveal. The illusion that there is a perennial return to a sort of federal-provincial balance has several causes. First, we do not normally draw distinctions between powers that orient or stimulate socio-economic change and plain administrative attributions, between creation and execution. Then we confuse occasional successes, confirmations of a provincial autonomy under threat, with the assumption of fresh prerogatives. Finally, we neglect the mutual effect of two key factors: historical acceleration and the enlarged role of government in today's society. These factors mean that the events of the last decade have considerably more impact in terms of the present and future evolution of federalism in Canada than all the preceding ones together.

The audit of a business enterprise looks at profits and losses for an entire year. Even if some months show a loss, it is possible for the business to have a profit for the year as a whole. The Canadian federal system is not a business, and must not be judged by methods applicable to private companies. The compensation effect does not automatically occur. Gains and losses, from the point of view of a province like Quebec, are not necessarily transposed by time. Quebec gains of ten, twenty, or seventy-five years back preserve their value only if they have not been annulled since and continue relevant today. More or less the same observation could be made of Quebec's losses. In this regard, even if one holds out against the evidence for recognition of a federal-provincial pendulum, Ottawa's action of recent years has led to such increase in the actual and potential powers of the central government that it is quite legitimate to ask if the Canadian federal system is not now committed irrevocably to centralization.

16
On to Ottawa:
The Logic of the System

Taking into account the forces that normally dominate the present system, must we view the centralization of major powers as irreversible? Yes, because the English-Canadian majority view it as rational and necessary. Moreover, it flows from the dynamic of Canadian federalism itself. Let us set aside the juridical subtleties, historical nuances, and divergences of opinion that are usually marshalled when we want to define Canadian federalism, and ask ourselves rather how the federation is understood by the average English-speaking Canadian. The fact is that he views it much more as an administrative structure than a political system designed, among other things, to protect the autonomy of provinces or safeguard a particular culture. Axiomatic, for this same English Canadian, is federal responsibility for issues of general importance affecting the collectivity as a whole. The province is expected to deal with questions of regional or local importance which have no effect beyond provincial frontiers; all others call for action by the central authority. To simplify further, let us say that English Canada views the federal government as the government of the nation, while the provincial government's powers are complementary and in general subordinate to those of Ottawa. English Canada believes that, ideally, the levels of public authority in a federal system pile up in a sort of pyramid with, at the very top, the government concerned with the country as a whole, the regional governments in the middle, and at the base, municipalities and local administrations. In the same way, the provincial order wields authority over the municipal, the federal enjoys the natural right of influencing provinces. At the top, the government of a country holds it as essential always to command the levers of power. Without them, that government is handicapped politically, financially, and administratively. In these circumstances it must take steps to restore its power, and no one can blame it for doing that.

In the other provinces and, of course, in Ottawa itself, the above is the current philosophy of federalism. It is virtually never expressed as I have put it here, but that does not mean it is any less present as a political reality in the minds of the people. Whatever species of angelic federalism optimistic Quebeckers may propose, English Canada remains staunch in its conviction that the country will survive in that it is led by a government endowed with substantial, varied, extensive, and unchallengeable powers. Whatever we may say, and whatever the juridical bases of the 1867 federation may have been, in short, the thing that matters now is what the majority of Canadians want to do with it.

We may conclude that the rest of Canada forgets certain subtleties to which Quebeckers are sensitive, or that the others are misinformed as to the exact juridical qualities of the Canadian federal system — 'Is Confederation an act or pact?' None of this speculation has much real significance in terms of the development of events. In other words, whether or not the majority English-Canadian idea or the minority French-Canadian idea is historically or juridically the right one is a question that loses its relevance as soon as the facts favour one or the other. And it cannot be denied that, at present, technology and the economy are working in favour of the opinion that would have the central power preponderant. Whether it ought to exist or not, centralization is now a necessity, at least for the majority of the people of Canada.

For English Canada, the mere fact of being Canadian involves a number of implicit requirements. One cannot belong to Canada and at the same time reject the limitations of adherence. This is as true for governments as for citizens. The federal or provincial authorities must face the effects of existence of the Canadian whole and accept the consequent responsibilities. Any other behaviour would be irrational. As a country Canada has 'national' objectives, confronts problems of 'national' importance, and must equip itself with 'national' means of action. Let us now look at some of the problems from the English-Canadian point of view to see how a country like Canada should normally be reacting to solve them.

If we have a crisis of unemployment, it is up to the federal authorities to implement such appropriate policies as they may decide on. It is also up to Ottawa to avoid provincial blocking of their effectiveness. As for the provincial governments themselves, their role is to co-operate with the central authorities and second Ottawa's effort. It would be inconceivable for them to oppose federal action or cancel its effects. In such a case the provincial régime would be working against the national objective of the fight against unemployment. At the same time, the federal administration should be regionalizing its policies as much as possible, and in this regard entrusting provinces with certain responsibilities they may more effectively discharge. If the provinces have any reason to think federal action inadequate, federal-provincial meetings afford them opportunities to inform Ottawa of this inadequacy. Altogether the general orientation and implementation of policy in the fight against unemployment is federal, with the provinces rounding off the picture, and co-ordination on both sides should distinguish the efforts made.

The same could be said for all powers which, in English-Canadian eyes, are connected with the economy, and they are numerous indeed. There are Quebec federalists whose outlook might seem similar at first glance, but they place far fewer issues in the economic category. Difficulty arises when the two lists are compared: for example, English Canadians see the income security programs as economic measures with social implications; for Quebeckers the reverse is true, and so forth.

Turning to the case of the fight against pollution, we note that the central government is not obliged to effect broad policies on its own. This can perfectly well be done by the provinces and municipalities, each working within its own area. But in a normal federation, not only is there nothing to stop the federal order from enacting standards for the whole country, and awarding financial support to provinces agreeing to conform to these, but in fact everything is stacked in favour of such a procedure. If the provinces were left to themselves, some would pass no environmental legislation at all, or else be less severe than others, perhaps in the hope of attracting industry. Thus the central authority must intervene, for reasons both of uniformity and its general responsibility for the quality of the environment. On what grounds can we oppose active concern with environmental quality on the part of the government of a federal country?

On what grounds can we, in a federation, deny the central government's right to active involvement in the citizen's standard of living? Why, in the area of income security, for example, or in hospitalization, or medical services, should it not be able to set minimum national standards, leaving it to provinces to offer better or more costly services as circumstances suggest? And why should not the central government itself send family allowance and pension cheques to citizens rather than leave it to ten provincial administrations, a procedure that would be less efficient and more expensive? Why, in fact, should the central government not become involved in the promotion of Canadian culture? If a Canadian nation exists, by what right can we prevent Ottawa from not only better mirroring this country's cultural diversity in its institutions and practices, but also giving financial and other support to the flowering of a Canadian culture?

For the past several decades we have seen staggering urban expansion. Canada is fast becoming one of the most urbanized countries on earth. This transformation of the milieu where so many Canadians work and play raises some very serious problems: clogging of transport systems, inadequate quality of housing, insufficiency of green space, finance in urban administrations, crime, and so forth. Why should the government of the country not be intimately involved in these issues? Several of the great cities of Canada are already economically and socially more important than some provinces. How is the job of solving these new urban problems to be left to provinces alone? It is certainly up to the country's government to take the necessary steps, in co-operation with provincial and municipal administrations. Who can argue with this necessity?

The need for scientific research requires no proof, and no advanced country can allow itself to neglect research without falling dangerously behind. Scientific research has become one of the basic conditions of technological and economic progress. How could the government of Canada ignore this fact on the pretext that it is in many cases closely linked with university teaching, and thus with education? The constant rise in prices in a country like Canada must inevitably move the central authority to action, and eventually to impose needed controls. What provincial government could find valid objection to this, since it has to do with the balance of the national economy and the standard of living of all citizens? Looking now at the flagrant disparities between one region of the country and another, is it not perfectly obvious that the federal government must intervene and assume a direct role in the stimulation of the inadequately developed regions?

This list could easily go on, but it is already enough for my purposes. We can now see the formidable obstacles facing any Quebec government loyal to federalism that set out to apply a brake, arguing from provincial autonomy or any other grounds, to extension of federal activity based on such obvious needs as these. The economic and social problems are genuine ones, affecting many citizens who are quite conscious of them. Many of the problems cannot be solved satisfactorily except by the use of the central government's powers, whether financial, juridical, or political. Moreover, for the reasons cited, virtually all the other provinces in the country would move instantly to call for some sort of federal intervention, or at least not offer much opposition to it. Finally, every 'national' government in the world is given responsibilities as extensive as those mentioned here.

Looking at this situation more closely, we can readily see that federal intervention based on the motives advanced in my list would lead, not to the temporary payment of auxiliary funds, but to a permanent federal presence in the areas affected. For the problems in my list are those present-day societies are facing. They did not exist either in this form or to this extent in the last century or even fifty years ago. There is nothing temporary about them. They call for a considered response, the results of which must then be carefully monitored. Nor have they anything in common with those natural disasters for which a generous subsidy is the sole and sufficient contribution expected of the higher government. Not only is the federal government itself inclined to accept the

responsibilities connected with these contemporary problems, but it is frequently egged on in this course by other provinces, public opinion, and the
example of other countries. In dealing with the fight against unemployment,
pollution, or poverty, in establishing national standards for social security, in
working directly with cities, in encouraging scientific research and taking part in
the costs of education, in playing an active role in cultural affairs or any other
area of general importance, the central government is guilty of none but quite
natural behaviour. It is discharging its duty as 'national' government and playing
the role expected of it; expected of it, at least, in English Canada.

The federal centralizing forces of the last century and our own time are hard
to evaluate side by side. In the past, the state's role was relatively modest, and
the federal-provincial struggle, or if one prefers the Quebec-Ottawa conflict,
developed within the political space established by the constitution and the ideas
of the day on the scope of government initiative, which was to be kept as
restricted as possible. Though not negligible in their effects, the state's policies
did not have the daily and often profound effect on individuals and society at
large that they later acquired. Today, whether we wish it or not, governments
are ubiquitous; no area of human life escapes the intervention or concern of the
state. In this sense, the significance of government decisions is incomparably
greater than before, and the political area of Quebec-Ottawa conflict too is much
enlarged, reaching out to embrace almost every imaginable sector of our lives.

The search for an even somewhat mutually exclusive division of legislative
powers is often viewed as the pursuit of a will o' the wisp. Almost everyone,
indeed, recognizes the close interrelation of public policies, both horizontal and
vertical: horizontal in the sense that decisions made by a government in one area
have repercussions in others for which the same authority is responsible, and
vertical in the sense that federal action has provincial side-effects, and vice versa.
The impossibility of reaching mutual exclusiveness in the distribution of
governmental responsibility is used by federalists as an argument for the absolute
necessity for intergovernmental co-ordination. They also use it to show that no
constitutional review, however careful and complete, will succeed entirely in
resolving Canada's federal-provincial problems; that the 'grey areas' will be
always with us.

All this is perfectly correct. It carries with it a corollary, however, to which
we have never paid enough attention; its consequences for the dynamic of
Canadian federalism are of tremendous practical importance. I have already said
that the Quebec autonomist ideology rejected centralization. Its proponents
believe in federalism, but they see it as perverted as soon as Ottawa shows the
slightest tendency to intervene in areas constitutionally reserved for provinces.
This federalist ideology has been broadcast with various degrees of emphasis by

virtually all Quebec political parties since Confederation. It has underlain the traditional Quebec stand in federal-provincial affairs. In the past few years it has prompted Quebec's insistence on a thorough re-examination of the BNA Act. In fact, the Quebec government had realized its inability to resist federal centralization. It was not always aware of the fact that this tendency to federal preponderance was only incidentally a result of constitutional imprecision, and arose much more immediately from the operation of such factors as the attitude of the rest of Canada and the nature of the problems of contemporary society. Thus, loyal to its autonomist and at the same time federalist thinking, the Quebec government issued the urgent call for a new constitution. When the process fell apart, some found consolation in saying that the present constitution was not so bad after all, since it had allowed substantial gains for Quebec in the Quiet Revolution. We now know what to think of these so-called 'gains.' Others decided that the affair was merely postponed, and discussion would be resumed at a more propitious time with more reasonable federal representatives. Still others believed the problems ought to be handled one at a time, so as to register gradual constitutional advance, hoping Ottawa would not have 'seen Quebec coming.'

This failure of the constitutional review is serious. It is serious particularly because a new Canadian constitution respecting the principles of division of powers announced in Quebec's briefs from 1968 to 1970 would certainly have been able to provide an acceptable basis for a new Quebec-Canada 'contract.' Such a constitution would have meant redefinition of the Canadian framework, and by helping to resolve it, recognized the political problem that had been Quebec's for generations, although emerging more overtly in the previous few years. The failure is serious also because it is hard now to see how it would be possible again to find as many energies and resources in federal and provincial circles as were mobilized from February 1968 until June 1971 for the attempted review program. Since the last Victoria meeting there has been no apparent interest in resuming talks either in Ottawa or in Quebec City. This is understandable. The memory of failure is still green in everyone's mind.

But this is not all. The miscarriage of the review, beyond the contribution certain uninterested, badly informed, or fearful Quebec representatives managed to make to it, is due basically to the fact that English Canada was not inclined to change its traditional view and understanding of the country and Quebec. It was unconvinced, in other words, of the need to go as far as Quebec wanted. It was not hostile, but acted naturally. It did not see the necessity of making profound changes to the division of powers between Ottawa and the provinces, or even between Ottawa and Quebec; it believed there was another way through, in terms of various accommodations not affecting anything it saw as basic to the present framework. When other Canadians had been informed that Quebec would think itself well off with a 'national' bilingualism policy in federal services, they could not see how it could insist on so profound an alteration in the country's structure.

English Canada has not been adequately informed of the stakes, it will be said, or the urgency of the review process called for by Quebec. And Quebec handled things badly. With this approach one can find all manner of explanations, some not utterly without grounds, to show that though the 1968-71 experiment failed the constitutional review Quebec wants is still a possibility. Is this really the case? If it must be embarked on in conditions similar to those prevailing from 1968 to 1971, the reply is negative. We may also presume that, as there has been a polarization of opinions in Quebec, a similar process will have occurred in English Canada and within the federal government before any resumption of constitutional review — with the difference, however, that English Canada will probably have become even more aware of the attributions which, in its view, should go to the federal government. This polarization ensures that nothing will arrest the tendency in the present system, natural and in harmony with federalism's dynamic as it is, towards centralization of the decisive powers of government. Strange though it may seem, no constitutional review carried out in the inherent conditions of this present system can now, despite all assertions to the contrary, effectively block the centralization movement. The factors that gave rise to failure will still be with us. When Quebec called for review, it was certainly not unaware of the possible strength of negative factors, but anticipated being able to neutralize them enough to get a satisfactory conclusion. We now know that such was not the case. Beginning again in similar circumstances would invite a similar result.

To be clearly understood here, let me first specify that this centralization is not a calamity of an automatic or mechanical sort. Constitutional review or no constitutional review, the process will not continue with sidereal regularity before a passive, impotent, or dumbfounded straggle of onlookers. There will be reaction. The centralization we are talking about is not simply a motion, but a process obeying the laws of politics. For this reason it will occur in stages, some rapid, others slow, some visible, others more veiled, according to the situation, and, obviously, given that the present system continues in force. At times, the more or less uninformed spectator of the Quebec-Ottawa scene will even think he is watching a wave of decentralization when it will really be nothing more than a momentary relaxation in the federal pull or else provincial assumption of functions Ottawa prefers to get rid of, either for administrative reasons or to lighten ballast. I have never claimed Ottawa wanted to do everything, but I do maintain that the federal government will want to take care of whatever it sees as important.

I know that the present constitution offers enough juridical possibilities and proven loopholes to back up federal action that erodes provincial power. If this constitution were partly changed — here and in what follows I am assuming a play of forces similar to 1968-71 — a fair number of possibilities would remain, enough in any event to leave the way open for the continuous growth of federal prerogative. Let us see, however, what new anti-centralizing guarantees could be built into a constitution completely remodelled in the circumstances indicated. It is an absolute certainty that neither Ottawa nor the other provinces would agree to a renovated Canadian constitution that did not expressly assign Ottawa those 'national' responsibilities which fall naturally, in their view, to the government of a country. Indeed, this is precisely why Ottawa would agree to reopen the review. From 1968 to 1971 the federal government took part in the exercise because of Quebec's insistence, but in future it will return to the task only if it sees a way to 'clarifying' powers, which means getting confirmation of a certain number of general powers in its own favour while resolving, again in its favour, the present uncertainty over the 'grey areas.' The English-speaking provinces will aim at protecting their present attributions, but not look for real increases in power. They will be calling for more revenue sources.

Even in the unlikely event of the rest of Canada's consenting to a special system for Quebec, it goes without saying that in exchange Quebec would have to steel itself to see Ottawa with extensive general responsibilities. Remember that I am talking about a new constitution for a Canada to which Quebec would continue to belong as a province. In this case, the federal government would obviously continue to exist, and at the time the new constitution was drafted all members of the federation, including Quebec, would agree to recognize important powers as belonging to Ottawa. If Quebec agrees to live within a federal system, it agrees logically not only to the existence but also to the functioning of federal power. As the other provinces and the English-Canadian majority want this power strong and not insignificant, and as they are committed to Canadian unity, it is unthinkable that all major responsibilities should not be assigned to the central government.

And what would these major responsibilities be? A clear idea of them can be obtained simply by referring to the list of questions a few pages back. The enumeration of possible federal attributions is neither detailed nor complete, but with the comments it contains, it gives a passably accurate approximation of the type of powers the government of Canada would be likely to secure for its own use in the new federal constitution I am discussing. These powers could give Ottawa all it needs to embark in any direction it sees as propitious politically. A constitution of this kind would in no way prevent decentralization of public administration in Canada, or more intensive provincial participation in the working out of broad 'national' policies. It could even give rise, if we want to be vastly optimistic, to a federalism some would describe as 'decentralized,' since provinces would undoubtedly continue to discharge various and massively-budgeted administrative functions as well as benefiting on occasion from financial transfers from Ottawa. The nine English-speaking provinces ask for nothing better; they have no nation to lead, and simply desire recognition as administrative entities, competent within their limitations and enjoying adequate financial means. But Quebec? Undeniably it would, like other provinces, be run from Ottawa, for it is in Ottawa and by the federal administration — with provincial participation or without it — that the broad future policies in every area of consequence would be massed. If Quebec were to enjoy a special system, an improbability at all events, this would certainly not extend so far as to allow it to accept or reject federal authority at will: in this respect it would be on the same footing as other provinces. Indeed its special system would begin and end with technical administrative arrangements, perhaps a little more numerous and more frequent than those affecting other provinces; it would surely not result in an increase of political power or legislative autonomy in relation to other provinces, even less in a special juridical status.

There is a basic logic in all this. Either Quebec accepts the rules of the present federal system or it rejects them. So far I have been assuming that Quebec accepted them. If in this spirit Quebec takes part in the making of a new constitution it certainly cannot expect its own unique, autonomist views to prevail; it will have to respect the opinions of Ottawa and the other provinces. In short, Quebec would have to compromise. Made in this manner, no new constitution could be effective for Quebec alone, and the result would have to include a certain number of restrictions, the most obvious of these being, in relation to Quebec's traditional political stand, confirmation of the central government's dominant role. This dominance cannot work in a vacuum. It must affect strategic areas that could not, in the perspective of a new constitution, be left to provinces, and which in any case nine Canadian provinces have no expressed desire to take on for themselves. To the extent Quebec agreed to be part of a federation governed by this new constitution, it could not turn later to arguments denying the system's basic characteristics. From time to time in recent years, Quebec has been able to do just that. The confused constitutional situation and the fluidity of circumstances allowed it. It was at least a good fight. But the day a new federal constitution was promulgated in a Canada of which it was a part, Quebec would have to bow to the natural restrictions involved. It would be all the more ill advised to adopt an attitude of challenge since it would itself have contributed to the drafting of the document, whether or not it was satisfied with the result. Any new federal constitution must originate in an overall commitment by its members.

We can now see how deceptive it would be for Quebec to hope a new constitution would win it more political power and, as Daniel Johnson had it, transform 'the Canada of ten into a Canada of two.' Federalists who see the document as the last chance for the Canadian federation fail to see that a Quebec government officially rejecting independence would actually put itself in a position of weakness; it would get virtually nothing in terms of increased power, or even confirmation of existing powers, if its partners know in advance that Quebec will never go so far as to seriously challenge the political system as such. And if it should do so, raising the 'threat of independence,' calling for changes that are seen as incompatible with a pro-federalist image or acting on its own in contravention of the laws of the system, Quebec either antagonizes the rest of the country and must then, if the review continues, negotiate with its credibility much reduced, or else, trapped in its own strategy, gradually becomes a government of independentist stamp. In this sense, the 'third way' that is supposed to lie somewhere between independence and unconditional federalism must eventually merge with one of the two others.

I have outlined what seems to be an irreversible tendency to centralization in Canadian federalism as it exists today. Is this tendency inherent in the political system as such? The judgement is hard to make. If the federal arrangement exists in a country dominated by a single cultural group, the centripetal forces will certainly meet fewer obstacles than if the country is made up of a number of ethnic groups, all of which are culturally and demographically viable. Canada's population is made up of two such viable groups, the English-Canadian group joined by most New Canadians, and the French-Canadian group centred in Quebec. This division explains the typical tendencies of Canadian federalism, and if we do not take it into consideration we cannot understand either federal-provincial tension in the country or the history of Canada altogether. In the Canadian system, the two societies naturally want to make use of the common mechanisms, that is the federal mechanisms, each to suit itself. Both aim to use the political environment for their own ends. We must not be surprised if the daily operation of this system, the rules governing it, and the objectives set for it, correspond more closely to the imperatives of the majority than to those of the minority. It is perfectly natural that this should be so. Occasionally, the English-Canadian majority will be moved to make concessions, but its power leaves me without hope that it will ever submit to structures, usages, and customs devised by and for the French-speaking minority. The minority, on the contrary, must submit to the majority in terms of the political institutions governing the whole. We have seen in this book how that universal rule applies in Canada.

17
The Government is Ourselves

I have said repeatedly that the Quebec government is an important collective instrument for the people of Quebec. Though there are various valid approaches and criteria for the evaluation of Canadian federalism, I have deliberately based my analysis on the idea of the powers of Quebec. Now I must turn back briefly to ask if I am right in giving such prominence to something that is, after all, only a political institution, and whether the establishment of an authentic government in Quebec City is really, as I have more than implied, an absolutely essential condition for the development and affirmation of Quebec society as a whole.

In our modern world, only those with economic, military, or political power manage to get their own way. Naturally, economic power counts for more than the others, and in this sense a number of multinational corporations wield greater influence than many sovereign nations. As for military strength, it generally goes hand in hand with economic strength. The political power too is that much greater if it is seconded by a solid industrial and technological plant with an abundance of capital. The case of the United States, or of the USSR, can leave us in no doubt on that point. As Quebeckers, we cannot and will never be able to make an impressive economic showing before the big powers. As far as military power goes, ours is non-existent, and with reason. Even independent, we could never hope to impose our wishes by arms as the Americans or Soviets have done and continue to do. Yet we still have a political lever, and it is the state of Quebec. Though it is imperfect, incomplete, circumstances give this political arm an exceptional importance for us in Quebec.

There is no indication that the recent tendency towards a growing state role in our daily lives is about to diminish. Some may be alarmed by this situation, and regret that we have come to tolerate an ever more penetrating governmental function. From many points of view they are right. It is tremendously important for state intervention in the years to come not to be technocratic or dehumanizing, but more attentive to the people's aspirations and, through new techniques of government, open to more active citizen participation. This said, I may add that Quebeckers are still 'lucky' to have a government. We may be comparatively poor in economic power, but the Quebec government exists. I have noted that governmental institutions are destined throughout the world to wield ever greater influence in our societies; thus, social, economic, and technological causes we have certainly not produced ourselves and over which we have no control are now operating to the advantage of the most powerful collective instrument we Quebeckers possess. The force of circumstance is lending it an active and decisive role that was certainly never foreseen or desired by the generations of Quebeckers that preceded us. In short we can take possession of this instrument at the very moment it is becoming worthwhile and, indeed, indispensable to our use.

Even if they see the enlargement of governmental activity as a real phenomenon, some federalists incline to the belief that the Quebec government's power, whether impressive or derisory, is a secondary strategic factor at a time when no government, strong in law though it might be, can truly do what it wants or, in other words, be genuinely autonomous. They wonder whether it is wise to place our bets on a political institution susceptible to the bonds of interdependence, particularly in the case of a small people such as ours. Rather than striving to build a Quebec power that is bound to be a delusion in any case, we would do better to secure the understanding and support of a government that is already solidly established, recognized as such by others, and working on solutions for such recent challenges as the growing interrelation between nations. As you have already guessed, this government is the federal. When various great blocs are forming all around the world, these federalists ask, is our desire to entrench and increase the powers of the government of Quebec a realistic one? Particularly in Europe, there are sovereign nations that are thinking of relinquishing some of the traditional elements of their sovereignty.

There is thus a whole school of thought to challenge the assertion that the state of Quebec may act as an essential lever for the collectivity. I have cited a few of the objections advanced. They fit together, since they all proceed from a particular viewpoint. Two basic notions emerge: one, the increasingly evident interdependence between countries questions the true effectiveness of any potential increase in the Quebec government's power, which is an anachronism anyway according to the federalist argument; two, in itself, political power offers no guarantee of the power of a nation.

For a very long time, rapprochement between nations was based largely on military considerations. Tactical alliances for conquest and defence have always existed, to be cemented or shattered at the will of king or emperor, but not necessarily reaching citizens in their daily lives. At present, such attempts at rapprochement, while not free of strategic motives, are based on economics more than on anything else, and may have the effect of diminishing a nation's sovereignty. Without going into all the subtleties, I may say that the old alliances were occasional, superficial, and often arbitrary, while the new ones are likely to go deeper; they will bring about real changes in the collectivities involved and they will be based on objective and calculable considerations. Princes used to make the alliances they wanted; future alliances will be dictated much more by a country's situation. Yet here and elsewhere in this work my intention is never to imply that the development of human society in general and the people of Quebec in particular depends on a vague determinism to which we individuals can only incline. We must be wary of such expressions as 'the flow of history.' It would be naïve to minimize the influence that can be worked on men's actions and their view of the world by such factors as better understanding of economics, reflection on the catastrophic consequences of modern warfare, interest in the protection of the environment and the improvement of the human milieu, concern with the standard of living, most, in short, of our contemporary trends of thought; they can help stir those currents occasionally seen in the behaviour of nations and individuals.

In obedience to such trends great world blocs are being formed, the best known being the European Common Market. The bloc begun in Canada in 1867 is still forming, and a similar process is occurring in a multitude of federations as well as among sovereign nations. There is no reason why we should not some day see a North American community that included the United States and Canada. There is little point in trying to foresee its characteristics; it is enough simply to point out that neither Canada nor the United States is immune to the forces at work for the integration of human communities. Will we then also see the establishment of a sort of international Confederation, a world government to which all countries would hand over a part of their sovereignty? It is really impossible to say. The world of tomorrow may assume shapes that are completely unexpected in terms of our experience. It is in this type of extrapolation, in fact, that we must beware of the so-called 'flow of history.' Though this coalescence may be dictated by economic forces, including the multinational corporations whose influence in state decision making must never be underestimated, the process is a result of governmental resolve. Given a necessary interdependence, governments seek advantage for their own populations. They remain as the ultimate and official architects of the political alliances the process involves.

It is taken for granted in today's Canada that the spokesman for the country as a whole is the federal government. It fulfils and will continue to fulfil this role as regards international debate arising from the imperatives of interdependence. The partial economic or political integration we may one day have to reach, with whatever other powers, will occur in accordance with terms accepted for the Canadian side by Ottawa, though we may presume some federal-provincial consultation. Yet there is an alternative. As a state, Quebec can equip itself to get the best possible deal in terms of a mutual dependence whose ineluctability and persistent development no one can deny. I have already said Quebec would benefit from aiming at a well-defined integration into Canadian federalism. It will have to be clear-minded enough to recognize the challenges of inter-dependence, and yet strong enough politically to ensure that this inter-dependence occurs in the conditions most advantageous for Quebec.

We may certainly expect Quebec to join any eventual North American bloc. But given the proper precautions, Quebec will go in without at the same time obliterating itself as a political and cultural entity. It will be one of the nations of the group, or bloc, and obviously not the most important one. If Quebec went in as part of a Canadian ensemble into which it would in a sense have melted politically, however, it would then be no more than one of the ethnic components of the group.

Two questions arise. 'Alone,' so to speak, against the United States, would Quebec be in a better negotiating position than it would be if it continued to benefit from federal protection? Considering the already advanced integration of the Canadian and American economies, neither Canada nor Quebec really has much room for manoeuvre in these terms, and can move only very gradually in the direction of greater economic autonomy. Looking at it another way, both Canada and Quebec are already subject to the penetrating influence of the American way of life, a process more marked in English Canada than in Quebec. We were asking about the economic protection that Quebec would get from a federal 'shield,' but in the past this shield has proven to be either powerless or simply not there. We are beginning to hear expressions of concern from all over Canada about the absence of firm federal policies in this area. This absence has worked largely in favour of American penetration. We are becoming more aware of it when the time for action is already very late, and when many and solidly entrenched private interests are profiting from it.

To the second question: if we assume that the present federal connection is preserved, should we assume also that the central government is bound to disregard Quebec interests in negotiating with the outside world? No, except that lacking a true state (and always on condition that it sustains an adequate demographic weight) Quebec will only be able to exert pressure on Ottawa through intermediaries and hope for the best. Few peoples in the world place their trust spontaneously in political institutions that they do not wholly control. Two certainties emerge as far as the people of Quebec are concerned: this inescapable interdependence is not so prejudicial a condition, providing we can participate directly in working out its modalities; and secondly, there is a corollary need, for this purpose, of a genuine government. In present and foreseeable circumstances, very few sovereign nations will adhere to a single bloc. If Quebec has to face the practical imperatives of its geographical location on the North American continent, this does not mean advance repudiation of a part in other blocs, for example the Francophone community. The world of the future will not be so compartmentalized as the 'cold war' may have led us to believe a few years ago. Relations among states will be multilateral, as they are increasingly even now. In other words, each will escape a little from its natural bloc affiliation and that includes Quebec, again providing it can itself decide how it will be interdependent and with whom.

Far from reducing differences between cultures and propelling them towards a formless fusion dictated by the 'flow of history,' the economic or political rapprochement of nations will prompt, in some cultures, a sort of defensive spasm With exceptions, these awakenings will not lead to renewal or revitalization of the culture unless it is already widespread — as the American culture is, for example — or involved in national collectivities whose private and public institutions will be solid enough to withstand this 'future shock.' In other cases, it is likely that after a brief awakening, the cultures will stop developing to survive only by a folkloric fixing process in the minds of their people. By no means all the so-called 'national' cultures will resist the coming of the interrelated world; some, it is impossible to tell how many, will find themselves no longer isolated and thus 'protected' in a world where frontiers will often be merely symbolic and where there will be an increased, many-faceted competition among the various cultures. This competition will become more noticeable and easier as more and more people gain access to education, the leisure civilization arrives, and the generalized use of means of communication we would not even have dared dream of a generation or two ago give the various cultures new means of mutual influence at the same time they give the most vigorous among them more effective potential for self-assertion and expansion than ever before. If we can take it for granted that political power in a democracy cannot and should not become the official cultural agent for the collectivity, we can also and increasingly take it for granted, given these possibilities of mutual influence, that political power can and will give increased weight to the culture, and influence the ways its people live and think. At the risk of being misunderstood in dealing with such a subject, I have to recognize the enormous potential impact of state action on a society's cultural processes. Of course, the state action I am talking about is not imagined as dictating the content and direction of the culture, as was the case with the 'socialist realism' so rampant in the USSR. I am thinking instead of that active interest of the public power as a support for the culture through financial measures and appropriate policies, and of the way in which this support is now viewed in most western countries.

Without the support of a genuine government, the Quebec culture could easily be one of those which, though valid objectively, will prove unresistant to the challenges of a world already forming before our eyes. This is one more reason why it is essential to have a Quebec government that is able to act. The aim here is not artificial protection for a moribund culture, but quite simply to give that culture, by means suited to circumstances, the possibility of enduring. So it is that the issue now, in economics as well as cultural affairs, is not one of cherishing some regressive design or trying to preserve a deceptive isolation, but of securing as complete a freedom as possible to decide for ourselves just how we are to be interdependent. What will count as far as the immediate future is concerned is not the supposed economic or cultural autarchy of peoples who cannot live without one another, but the concrete and daily expression of an interrelation to which all nations will be subject. In the world that has already begun, independences will no longer be proclaimed, but negotiated. In this type of market, Quebec must be present in its own quality; otherwise the chances are that it will be absent in this sense for ever. And its most natural spokesman cannot be other than its own government.

Up to now I have been arguing a little as if Quebec's possession of a true government would automatically make it powerful, and capable of impressing partners in future negotiations. Should we conclude that political strength is decisive in itself? That it is superior to all other influences that may bear on a negotiation? Certainly not. There are many peoples with autonomous governments who are still weak. Some sovereign nations are utterly incapable of defending their interests as they would wish. In certain cases, especially in the smallest countries, we have witnessed the emergence of politically sovereign colonies in this past generation.

There is no cause-and-effect relation between political independence and power when we are referring to medium or small nations. It is a fact that few thinking people will question. However, if political independence does not necessarily confer power, unrestricted dependence certainly produces impotence. To turn to metaphor: education does not mean that all educated people will succeed in life, but ignorance in our own time is more and more a cause of failure; the better educated a person is, the better equipped he is to meet today's requirements in the labour market. In the same sense, a people with its own government is not assured of success in all its endeavours or even most of them, but a people without a true government and the strength it confers, however minimal, is seriously at a loss when the time comes to argue its general interests. The question is basically one of equipment — individual in the case of education, and collective in the case of government.

What I am claiming, then, is that the people of Quebec must be equipped if it wants to be heard with respect. Its individual members must also be equipped individually with what they need in terms of education, health, minimum income, and so on. But in any ordered society, services to individuals and services to the collectivity do not come separately. The government's role is not simply external. It must continue to exercise responsibilities of management and especially of direction in the community from which it emanates. This is its internal role, more continuous in impact and more decisive in the development of the society than its external role. This means that even without an external role, an authentic Quebec government will still be an internal necessity. If I had to examine this subject from the viewpoint of the last century, I would be ill advised to give so great an importance to the influence of the public powers. Other institutions then played for Quebeckers the role presently played, and likely to be played for some time to come, by their government. If, on the other hand, I had to write this analysis a few centuries from now, when socio-economic systems are liable to be quite different from what we know today, I might have to focus my attention on institutions other than government to find those in the best position, at that moment, to serve as instruments for the collectivity.

I must now be specific as to why what is true for Quebec is not necessarily true for the other provinces in Canada. Have their citizens not as much need as Quebeckers for a government of their own? The answer to this is that they have it already, with no indication that they will be deprived of it in the years to come. This government is in Ottawa. In an earlier chapter, we saw how the Quebec-Ottawa relation differs fundamentally from the Ontario-Ottawa, Saskatchewan-Ottawa, or New Brunswick-Ottawa relation. It will suffice to add here that despite certain differences in viewpoint or thinking among residents of other provinces, they possess no cultural differences among themselves as marked as those separating them all from Quebec. It is true, as some superficial observers always insist, that each province in Canada differs from the others, but they forget Quebec is in a separate category and in it alone. From this point of view, the people of Quebec constitute a very distinct community in Canada and one to which no other community in the country can really be compared. This

Quebec community is the beginning and end of a long history of special institutions, a language heard largely on Quebec territory, and a persistent desire to safeguard its integrity in the fullest sense of that term.

And why should we set so much store by this way of being, this culture? The question has no really satisfactory technical answer. There is no strictly rational way of evaluating human aspirations as natural as those that ultimately explain the 'Quebec problem.' Some communities simply persist in wanting to preserve and improve the identity that with time, and sometimes in the face of circumstance, they have managed to form. In these cases, the instinct for survival and affirmation is immeasurable: it is simply present as a historical fact worthy of respect and sometimes even of admiration.

18
Conclusion: The Present Imperative

As soon as I begin to look at possible solutions for the 'Quebec problem' I inevitably think of the various political opinions that have been mobilizing defenders and adversaries over the past decade or so: more or less centralized federalism, more or less special status, sovereignty-with-association, and separatism. The variants are numerous, and even more numerous the meanings given them by any group of citizens. In these last pages, then, I will prefer to stick to a line of thinking that suits my overall approach better than a detailed study of the range of possibilities from the status quo to total independence.

Whatever one's opinion on how the 'Quebec problem' might be resolved, it must relate to one of two basic and mutually exclusive choices: the Canadian choice or the Quebec choice. I have no intention here of straying into a species of shallow political Manichaeanism, but hope to draw a few clear conclusions from an objective examination of the facts. As I have tried to show in this book, the Canadian choice, which involves acceptance of the present Canadian environment with its federal system and the balance of forces and rules that typify that system, is visible and concrete. The reality in which it exists imposes certain standards, certain behaviour, and also certain political restrictions. Like federalism itself, the Canadian choice does not exist in a readily idealizable universe of the abstract, but in an observable and highly measurable daily world. Make the Canadian choice and you automatically get the whole package. This would be true even if we managed to adjust some aspects of the current Canadian system to Quebec's needs, for though it might be slowed down, the system's dynamic would still be at work, and lead us in the long term to the identical destination. On the other hand, the Quebec choice — the decision to give Quebec's own government ultimate leadership in Quebec affairs — is the only consistent and lasting way of removing the centralizing pressure of Canadian federalism and its natural result, the demise of the political power of Quebec.

A Quebec administration of federal loyalties can always offer momentary resistance to the process and make a show of force: double taxation, unauthorized attendance at international conferences, unilateral decisions, and so on. This kind of government may also sometimes boycott federal-provincial mechanisms. However, these tactics, in a government of federal loyalties, could never emerge as normal behaviour — or even an effective negotiating technique, for any 'gains' made in this way, supposing for one moment that a show of force achieved anything at all, would undoubtedly prompt an eventual counter-offensive from Ottawa. Finally, there is no reason to think intergovernmental guerrilla warfare should develop as the normal way of conducting public business in an orderly federation. Being part of a federation without wanting to be subject to the restrictions it imposes is at best a political absurdity, and at worst, gross misrepresentation.

As a result, a Quebecker has but two positions open to him. He must make either the choice for Canada or the choice for Quebec. Our regard for prudence or moderation or balance must no longer keep us in those middle ways of that whole period when we had not yet been shown, by the commotion of more recent years and the evolution of party politics in Quebec and Ottawa, where they were taking us. We can be satisfied no longer with formulas such as 'two nations,' 'two societies'; 'co-operative,' or 'paying,' or 'decentralized,' or 'true' federalism; 'special status,' 'equality or independence,' 'renewed Confederation,' 'cultural independence in economic federalism,' and so on. We can see on closer examination that these formulas and any others that might yet be invented simply confuse the choice to be made and put off the time of choosing; they give us vague ideas or electoral slogans while the federal system keeps functioning, untroubled and, one might say, without troubling itself.

Sooner or later, the choice for Canada involves submission to unconditional federalism, leading to centralization. Those making this their choice, even when they anticipate the maintenance of a strong and effective Quebec administration, must logically recognize in the country's government, and hence in the central government, some responsibility for the economic, social, cultural, and political orientation of Quebec: the Canadian choice would not otherwise exist. They cannot, therefore, oppose federal action flowing from this responsibility. And federal activity will grow more and more extensive and influential as the possibilities of governmental action are developed and refined. Eventually, first for purposes of co-ordination and later to ensure comparable services for all Canadians, Ottawa will be setting standards in every area of 'national' interest and originating all general policies.

As for the Quebec choice, in which the orientation of our society would come from Quebec City with Ottawa's contribution seen as auxiliary, it must, if we are to translate it into reality, lead to the search for independence. We have already seen how the Canadian group opposes Quebec's autonomist views, especially as regards the division of powers. The continued existence of these views within the federal system would have two simultaneous results, something, moreover, that has been observed already: repeated rejection of these views accompanied by a succession of Quebec-Ottawa clashes that grow more and more numerous, harassing, and expensive in time, energy, and money.

If, despite all this, the proponents of the Quebec choice persist in advancing it within the present political structure, Ottawa will succeed in the long term, through a process of tactical and then obligatory concessions from Quebec, in separating the Quebec government from its most valuable prerogatives, and cancelling out such gains as may occasionally be made either by shows of force or in exceptional circumstances. I have shown in preceding chapters how Canadian federalism can achieve this end through its own natural action and the intrinsic tendencies of the system. In short, operating within the federal framework and using the traditional techniques of federal-provincial negotiation, partisans of the Quebec choice will wear themselves out, soon to be left with nothing but the hope of passing on to succeeding generations their ever diminishing hope of one day changing a reality over which they exert less and less control.

The Quebec choice and membership in the Canadian federal system as we know it are henceforth irreconcilable objectives. The two could co-exist in the past, since federal and Quebec powers were less in contact. Today they overlap; tomorrow will overlap more. In a country with federal and provincial governments the effective performance of government and the welfare of the citizens require, here as elsewhere, that there be only one political institution with the decisive legislative and administrative power, and that the authority of this power be unchallengeable. Otherwise, if both orders have comparable powers, if they share certain powers in neighbouring sectors, if neither government has general ascendancy over the other, we may find them both, for reasons of prestige, votes, or common rivalry, advancing contradictory measures and cancelling one another out in ceaseless bickering even if neither has any real desire to act. Whatever we think, it would be totally deceptive in such a case, as experience has shown us, to place our faith in consultation and co-ordination. This is not how to rid ourselves of anarchy. There was a danger of mutual cancellation in Canada when the Quebec of the Quiet Revolution managed to disturb the federal-provincial balance, however slightly and momentarily. Later, Ottawa regained the offensive to reaffirm its authority. The reaction was natural in terms of the present system, and the federal authority will ultimately emerge unchallenged by all governments in the system. There will be a new federal-provincial balance; in it, provincial governments will have numerous responsibilities, but they will be local and regional in nature. Among other things, they will have the jobs of adapting the broad policies set by the central government to local conditions and overseeing the administration of well-established programs. These governments will certainly continue to be important in terms of budget and managerial function — perhaps even more important than is now the case — but preparation for the near and distant future, and hence the general orientation of society, will be seen as an entrenched federal responsibility.

If one chooses the present federal system and also wants to avoid the waste of time, money, and energy, as well as intergovernmental conflict; if within that system, one wants citizens to derive the greatest possible material benefit from policies that may not have been invented in Quebec and for Quebec, but which may at the same time not be all that bad, one must — and this then amounts almost to a duty to one's fellow citizens — reject the choice for Quebec and agree like other Canadians to 'play the game' whatever its rules may be; rally to the choice for Canada, satisfied simply to hope for the enlightened, sympathetic, and — why not? — humanitarian and paternalistic understanding of the English-Canadian majority towards the community of Quebec. This may not be the most meritorious route for a people, but it is surely the easiest. It does no harm. It even offers advantages, at least for as long as English Canada's patience and sympathy last. It kills no one, but helps in the quiet extinction of a nation. Although certain, the procedure is painless, its progress scarcely noted from one year to the next. In fifty or a hundred years, French-speaking Quebeckers will still exist, of that we may be sure; there are still many Ukrainian and German speakers in the western provinces. They are good Canadians, as everyone recognizes. Quebeckers can, like them, become good Canadians. They have only to let it happen. The choice for Canada is extremely plausible.

Successive Quebec governments have, however, stuck with the choice for Quebec. They have defended it with varying intensity, of course; they have worked out its various elements with more or less rigour. Circumstances, the lack of political courage, or susceptibility to deceptive short-term strategies — all of these regular by-products of the federal scheme of things — have caused some governments to set this commitment temporarily aside. No Quebec government, however, has ever emerged as the articulate and compelling champion of the choice for Canada and everything that choice implies. All have at least moved within the orbit of the Quebec choice, and several have clarified what that choice means; yet none has been able or has wanted as a government to carry through to the logical conclusion of the reasoning and options underlying the choice. In any event, there was a long period when such a final commitment would have been premature.

If we want the choice for Quebec to be translated into reality, it is essential for us to break the vicious federal circle, bring down the roadblocks with which we are faced in the present Canadian political system. The circle cannot be broken by the methods of the past; in the context of present-day federalism we cannot expect to find exits that do not and cannot exist if the system is faithful to its own nature. In the Canadian context, the choice for Quebec is a contradictory factor, a source of frustration and problems; it is a graft that is and must be rejected by the political organism if the latter is to ensure its own effectiveness and survival. Nevertheless, it also offers us the ideal that is likeliest to rally Quebeckers around a single objective and end the divisions and ambiguities now afflicting them. The vicious circle of federalism will be broken by Quebec public opinion, on condition only that this opinion focus on the quest for Quebec independence, the democratic means of achieving it, and the economic and social reforms for which it will be the key as well as the prior condition. The real danger for the Quebec nation is not in independence but in submission to political forces that lead it now and will in future lead it increasingly to behave as a cultural minority on its own ground.

The independence here envisaged is no autarchy, which at all events would be an illusion in this modern world. It is far from a withdrawal into ourselves. It does not mean the overturning of all Quebec's established values, or of those values current in the North American world where Quebec lives and will continue to live. Independence does presuppose, however, that as far as Quebeckers are concerned, the government of Quebec holds all the political powers. This certainly does not preclude setting up and pursuing mutually beneficial relations with Canada; but it is Quebec, and not influences that come from outside and are often foreign to its interests, that will itself direct, as other sovereign nations of the world manage to do, the elements of its development and self-affirmation.

The necessity of Quebec's political independence can be argued on the basis of many considerations other than those advanced in this book. I decided to focus my own analysis on the functioning of the Canadian federal system because in political circles, and in Quebec society in general, its true nature is unknown.

Expressions of independence may be as varied as the ways of proving its necessity; its detailed working out must involve a whole series of concerns which do not come within the scope of the present work. The economic, social, and cultural objectives to accompany Quebec's arrival at independence form a natural part of the platform of an independentist party. It also falls to this party to decide on the role of the state in a sovereign Quebec, and on the new modes of governmental behaviour which will draw heavily on citizens and private institutions. The government is an essential instrument, but it must not become altogether ubiquitous.

The need for independence is harder to pin down when we look for absolute motives. Those peoples with choice and sufficient self-awareness furnish themselves with the collective instruments that suit them. They often do this by instinct. They may also do it after careful thought, in full command of the facts.

It is as a contribution to the thinking of the people of Quebec that this book has been written. The writer's only wish is that, whatever the route they choose, it is chosen in the light of reality, with knowledge of the facts — facts of the past, present, and the foreseeable future.